D1403466

Tracing the Footsteps of God

Discovering What You Really Believe

C. S. Song

Fortress Press
Minneapolis

TRACING THE FOOTSTEPS OF GOD
Discovering What You Really Believe

Library of Congress Cataloging-in-Publication Data
Song, Choan-Seng, 1929-
  Tracing the footsteps of God : discovering what you really believe / C.S. Song.
     p. cm.
  Includes index.
  ISBN 978-0-8006-3892-4 (alk. paper)
  1. Theology, Doctrinal—Popular works. I. Title.
  BT77.S68 2007
  230—dc22   200700294

Cover design by Brad Norr; Cover photo © Image Source/Corbis. Used by permission.
Book design by Michelle L. N. Cook

The paper used in this publication meets the minimum requirements of American National Standard for Information Sciences—Permanence of Paper for Printed Library Materials, ANSI Z329.48-1984.

Manufactured in the U.S.A.

11   10   09   08   07   1   2   3   4   5   6   7   8   9   10

Contents

Introduction

From Where Shall We Start and How Shall We Proceed?

Some years ago an American boy boarded an airplane in New York. He thought he knew where he was going. After an unusually long flight the plane finally landed, but upon entering the airport the boy was totally confused. Things didn't seem quite right. And things were not quite right. The boy had expected to be in Oakland, California. He was, however, in Auckland, New Zealand. He had boarded the wrong airplane. Call it a journey gone awry, a perfect example of the Chinese proverb, "A slight error in the beginning results in a big mistake in the end."

Starting a theological journey of exploration with the wrong question is like heading to Oakland on the wrong airplane. In either case, you're unlikely to reach your destination.

What's the Wrong Question? God

How, then, should we go about the exploration of religious faith? What are the questions to be addressed and in what order should they be asked if our journey of exploration is not to go awry? For most Christian faith traditions and schools of Christian theology, the question of God is the beginning point. And yet, when we think of the whole matter more deeply, we may realize that this time-honored way of doing theology parts company with the methods of science and technology. Science seeks to discover what is presently unknown by the study of what is known. God is a great unknown. To begin with God, therefore, is to attempt to explain what is known by way of what is not known, quite the opposite of how science proceeds. Rather we should begin where we are with what can be known through our experience in the world and see where it takes us.

We will begin in each chapter, therefore, by approaching the ultimate with questions, problems, and concerns that arise from our experience of penultimate things. We will start with what we know, or imagine we know, from our experience and the questions our experience gives rise to. We will then dip into narratives from within—and from without—the Christian tradition. We will want to know whether and how these narratives, drawn from the panhuman quest for religious/spiritual understanding, shed light on our own questions. Each chapter will contain several questions for further thought that attempt to reframe the question, problem, or concern we started with in such a way that we are encouraged to keep asking questions.

And we will pay attention to Jesus of Nazareth whose life and teaching, death, and resurrection are, as it were, a window onto the God we are seeking to know, understand, and experience. In so doing, we hope to share in Jesus' deep God-consciousness. As the reality of who and how we are encounters the reality of who and how Jesus was, our perception and understanding of God continually deepen and our questions, consequently, continually change.

German poet Rainer Marie Rilke's advice to a young poet is good advice for a young (or even an old) theologian as well: "Be patient toward all that is unsolved in your heart and try to love the questions themselves, like locked rooms and like books that are now written in a very foreign tongue. . . . Live the questions now. Perhaps you will then gradually, without noticing it, live along some distant day into the answer."

Here, then, are the questions that we will love—and hopefully learn to live—as we move through the chapters of this book:

1. What about Beginnings and Endings?
2. Did Jesus Rise from the Dead and Does It Matter?
3. Healing or Saved? Or Both?
4. All Roads Lead to Rome?
5. How Can We Know God and What God Wants?
6. What Is the Church?
7. What Is Christian Mission?
8. What Is Spirituality?
9. What Do You Say God Is?

With these questions we set out on a journey that will take us through the heart of the world we inhabit into an encounter with God—a journey that will lead us to a vision of the God who is beyond our life and history but who, at the same time, is at work in our life and history.

Keep in mind as you set out on this journey that the purpose of our exercise is not to come up with *correct* answers to the issues posed and the questions raised. As a matter of fact, we may not find neat and elegant answers to many of them. It is our hope that as we wrestle with them honestly, we may be led to a deeper understanding of who we are and to a personal encounter with that loving power we call God—from whose eternity we came and to whose eternity we return.

1. What about Beginnings and Endings?

At the stroke of midnight a new day begins and an old day ends. At the next stroke of midnight, that day ends to herald the beginning of yet another new day. Our time is made up of countless beginnings and endings. We know that; we've all experienced it; we usually don't think about it.

Whether we are mindful of it or not, everything, including our life and the history of peoples and nations, begins at a certain point in time and also ends at a certain point in time. There is no beginning that does not have an ending; nor is there an ending that does not pave the way for the beginning of something else.

"There is no feast under heaven that has no end," says a Chinese proverb. In American culture we might say there is no Super Bowl party that has no end. We should not take such sayings as mere expressions of passing sentiment. They have a much deeper meaning; they evoke in us perhaps inarticulate feelings of sadness; they give rise to a sense of resignation and perhaps anxiety, if not fear. "There is no feast under heaven that has no end." The saying captures the perception of time as temporal and transient. The "feast," of course, is a metaphor. You could just as well say that there is no fame, position, fortune, or anything else that has no end. The inference is clear: life is short-lived. It does not last forever.

In a similar vein, another Chinese idiom states, *"The music is over and the people are gone."* Again we confront the transience of human experience. Who has not been to a concert? When the music begins, the place is filled with people, but when it is over no one remains. The performance inspires a wide range of immediate, intense feeling, but then *"the music is over and the people are gone."* The saying conveys both a recognition of, and a sadness over, the short-lived nature of human experience and surfaces deep feelings of anxiety. This is how we live our lives—between beginnings and endings, listening for the music to end and send us away. But to where? To a final ending that makes a mockery of all our beginnings?

The book of Ecclesiastes in Hebrew scripture gives us a magnificent poetic expression of the human condition, of the temporality and transience of human experience. "For everything," we are told, "there is a season, and a time for every matter under heaven." Then follows a litany of images that resonate with the experience of every man and every woman. In crisp, pithy, almost unrelenting language, the author states what should be obvious to those who care to notice and think about it. [There is:]

> a time to be born, and a time to die;
> a time to plant, and a time to pluck up what is planted;
> a time to kill, and a time to heal;
> a time to break down, and a time to build up;
> a time to weep, and a time to laugh;
> a time to mourn, and a time to dance . . .
> (Ecclesiastes 3:1–4)

The litany goes on, but the point is made. Nothing lasts. Do you not wonder whether God has anything to do with such beginnings and endings? Do you not wonder how to think about eternity when our experience is wholly within the temporal and transient?

There is indeed "a time to be born, and a time to die." You were born at a certain time on a certain day in a certain year. You were not conscious of it when you were born, but your mother knows exactly the time you were born. You are fully alive in this present moment as you read this book, but your death is waiting for its time. You are mortal, and there will be a "time to die." We all know it, even if we would prefer not to think about it. In truth, one day *the music will be over and the people will be gone.*" Such reflections surface the deep existential anxiety of those who live between beginnings and endings and so suggest an excellent beginning point for our journey toward God.

Narratives of the Beginning

For the music to be over, however, it must have a beginning. Beginnings matter. As we raise our eyes to look at the stars and the moon in the dark sky, we wonder about their birth millions upon millions of years ago. We are told by science of the theoretical possibility that there exist many universes, and we wonder about their beginnings. We are wondering about creation, the beginning of all beginnings.

"Creation" is the all-encompassing word for all that is and exists. From universes to galaxies to solar systems, from suns and moons to planets, from mountains to seas to trees, birds, animals, men, and women, we are all creatures, all part of the creation. Creation confronts us with an important question. As the German theologian, Paul Tillich, once asked, "Why is there something rather than nothing?" Who gave birth to all that is? The ancients struggled with this question; we struggle with it. The great creation myths of humankind are an attempt to breach the ineffability of this question.

The Hebrew Story of the Beginning

The first of the Hebrew stories of creation begins with a profound sense of transcendence, of the extraordinary feat of God, the one who speaks creation into existence.

> In the beginning when God created the heavens and the earth, the earth was a formless void and darkness covered the face of the deep, while a wind from God [or the Spirit of God] swept over the face of the waters. Then God said, "Let there be light"; and there was light. (Genesis 1:1–3)

What is this "beginning" at the very outset of the creation story? It is an absolute beginning, absolute in the sense that this is the beginning that begins all other beginnings, be it of a universe or a life on earth. We cannot go behind this beginning. If you insist that there must be something prior to this absolute beginning, you should reflect on the fact that the human mind cannot escape the temporality that began with this beginning. Look at the stars as the ancients did, and perhaps you will hear as they did the universe declaring: "In the beginning, God!" We can go no further. The Hebrew creation story makes no attempt to get behind the "beginning." Rather it celebrates the beginning and praises the God who creates.

Psalm 104, a hymn to creation and its creator, is a case in point. It begins with praise and adoration to God the creator:

> Bless the Lord, O my soul,
>   O Lord my God, you are very great.
> You are clothed with honor and majesty,
>   Wrapped in light as with a garment. (Psalm 104:1–2a)

To celebrate creation is to celebrate God and to celebrate God is to celebrate the creation God has made. Psalm 104 is grounded in the faith that creation did not just happen. God made it happen. God made the beginning begin. The doxological opening of the psalm is followed by a poetic account of how God carried out the work of creation:

> You [God] stretch out the heavens like a tent,
>   you set the beams of your chambers on the waters,
> you make the clouds your chariot,
>   you ride on the wings of the wind. . . .
> You set the earth on its foundations,
>   So that it shall never be shaken. (Psalm 104:2b–5)

The poet then goes on to describe in graphic images how God caused all things to come into being and cares for all things. Creation is, the poet insists, a window on God. Perception of the wonder of creation evokes the mystery of God and leads to praise and adoration:

> I will sing to the Lord as long as I live;
> I will sing praise to my God while I have being.
> (Psalm 104:13)

The authors of the Genesis creation story and Psalm 104 move from what they know immediately—creation—to what they cannot know immediately—God. Their perspective on the world is informed by their faith in God, their trust in a God who creates and sustains. Their faith has reached the beginning behind which it cannot go.

No more questions are asked. Neither is any doubt expressed. As long as God was in command of the beginning, there is no need for us to look back. All we have to do is to look forward with confidence grounded in such faith.

A Hindu Narrative of the Beginning

Faith, that is trust, in the God of the beginning, seems to have developed among our ancestors in most places. The creation hymn from the Rig Veda, ancient scriptures of India dating as far back as 1500 B.C.E., is a good example:

> Then even nothingness was not, nor existence.
> There was no air then, nor heavens beyond it.
> What covered it? Where was it? In whose keeping?

The theological concerns here parallel those in Genesis. This writer also makes it clear that the beginning of creation is an absolute beginning, the beginning of all beginnings. The poet of the Rig Veda is from a religious culture very different from that of either the writer of Genesis 1 or the poet of Psalm 104, but he seems to share a similar religious concern. He too is interested in the origin of the temporal world we live in.

> The One breathed windlessly and self-sustaining.
> There was that One then, and there was no other.
> At first there was only darkness wrapped in darkness.
> All this was only unillumined water.
> That One which came to be, enclosed in nothing,
> arose at last, born of the power of heat.
> In the beginning desire descended on it
> that was the primal seed, born of the mind.

The language of this scripture from ancient India curiously resembles the Genesis creation story. The religious faith contained in these verses reflects a deep sense of awe for "the One" who made the beginning of all things, just as the creation story in the Hebrew Bible did in relation to God the creator.

To know this "One" is to know all things, and all things lead back to this "One" as their source. Beyond this, little can be said. We come again to the beginning behind which we cannot go, and so this ancient hymn of creation turns into a confession of both ignorance and trust.

> But, after all, who knows, and who can say
> Whence it all came, and how creation happened?
> The gods themselves are later than creation,
> So who knows truly whence it has arisen?
> Whence all creation had its origin,
> He, whether he fashioned it all or whether he did not,
> He, who surveys it all from highest heaven,
> He knows or maybe even he does not know.[1]

"Whence all creation had its origin" the One who "fashioned it all" knows, and like the Hebrew writers, the Indian poet is content to leave the origin of creation to the One. He has no choice; he has reached the limits of human imagination and intellect. The poet's acknowledgement of the boundaries of human thought is expressed humorously in the final two lines quoted above. Perhaps this little piece of "theological humor" is his way of expressing faith in the "One," as well as joy in the creation and in the mystery of its creator.

We, like the ancients, must leave the question of the origin of creation to the "One," to God the creator. Our minds stop where theirs did. Paul Tillich's question, "Why is there something rather than nothing?" can only be answered, "God." So we give that answer and then move on to questions suggested by these ancient narratives that we can grapple with:

1. Does it make psychological sense to answer Tillich's question by saying, "God"?

2. If you accept "God" as the answer to Tillich's question, are there any grounds for faith/trust in a creator God? (You might want to look carefully at Psalm 104 in reflecting on this question.)

3. How could trust in a creator God be expressed in both personal and communal spiritual contexts?

4. If you posit a creator God as the origin of all material and temporal reality, what would that imply about the relationship between human and non-human realities?

5. How would faith/trust in a creator God inform both personal and communal ethics?

Many more questions will, no doubt, be raised as a result of bringing your own experience into contact with these and other ancient creation narratives. And, tending to these questions of the "beginning" will, no doubt, begin to surface questions about the "end."

Narratives of the End

The beginning of creation is behind us; the end of creation looms threateningly before us. When it comes to the end of our world and our universe, not to mention ourselves, most of us, if not afraid, are at least anxious. In descending order, the possibility that the creation, the world, the tribe/nation, the individual might be destroyed is a panhuman, and thus pan-religious, concern. Will nothing be the final word? Literally nothing—no sound, no color, no smell, no movement, even no shadow, nothing. Will nothing become nothing? Here the mind can go no further. Final ending, like first beginning is impenetrable. First beginning and final ending contain and limit temporal experience. That, of course, does not stop us from wondering.

As it was with the ancients, when our minds move toward the absolute end, they move toward dread. The threat of extinction at any level leads to a deeply "existential anxiety" and without our always knowing it, most of what we do is a struggle against, or denial of, this deep-rooted anxiety.

A Flood Narrative from Taiwan

I suspect existential anxiety over the threat of extinction underlies the many great flood myths told by our ancestors in many cultures. The flood story of the Amis, the largest of some dozen tribes that have been inhabiting the little island-nation of Taiwan for thousands of years, is a case in point:

> Long, long ago, there was an island called Lagasan in the middle of the ocean. This couple (ancestors of the Amis) had two children. The son was named Doci and was fourteen years of age; he had a younger sister called Lalatan. She was not over two years of age. One day, it was time for the crops to be harvested.
>
> "My son, we, your parents, have no time to attend to the farm over the mountains. You have to take good care of your sister and go to our farmhouse on the other side of the hill. After getting there, let the rice just harvested yesterday dry by spreading it out on the area of the threshing floor in front of the shelter. All of the crops were stored near the canoe."
>
> After getting to the temporary shelter in the fields, Doci started drying the rice and the millet because the sun was shining brightly. No sooner had he finished drying them than it became darker and darker. Alas! After the lightening came the thunder, and it started pouring rain. It happened so quickly, all Doci could do was pick up his younger sister and get in the canoe.

The whole area was destroyed by the flood. Everything happened suddenly, frightening these poor children. Both of them lost consciousness for several days before they found themselves afloat in the ocean with a lot of things, which the Amis have thenceforth lived on for thousands of years, betel nut, breadfruit, and a kind of persimmon. . . .

After some days, they ran out of the food Doci had brought into the canoe. . . . Luckily, it seems Doci heard birds singing in the trees in his dream, and he woke up all of a sudden. He could not believe they were on the seashore. He jumped up and went out to search for some food near the seaside. How excited he was![2]

Ancient flood stories from different cultures may differ in the details; however, as has been noted, "the flood narrative like the creation narrative is part of the common property of humanity."[3] Flood narratives contain "humankind's basic expression of its being-in-the-world, of the threat to human existence."[4]

In the Amis's story of the flood, the lives of the two children were in mortal danger. The story tells us that they lost consciousness for several days, a metaphor for the threat to their existence. There is far more at stake, however, than the continuing existence of these two children. On their existence depends the existence of their people, their village, their world, even the creation. The children must be saved. The canoe, just as the ark in the biblical story of the flood, has to be provided to save not only the children but the creation itself from extinction. We are faced with a circular threat, the threat that our death could be the end of all and that the end of all could be our death.

The Hebrew Narrative of the Flood

There is no hint in the Amis's story of why the existence-threatening flood occurred. It just happened. *What matters in the story is that life continues in spite of the threat of extinction.* This invites us to look at the biblical story of the flood in a different light. The Genesis story provides a reason for the flood—God's decision to make an end of "the human beings I have created—people together with animals and creeping things and birds of the air," because "the wickedness of humankind was great in the earth . . . (Genesis 6:5, 7). Creation itself is not mentioned or threatened, only living creatures face the prospect of extinction. Therein is the heart of existential anxiety, and it is that anxiety that the story addresses. In the face of the unknowns, uncertainties, and ambiguities of existence, what matters is that life continues in spite of the threat of extinction.

Noah, his family, and the living creatures who entered the ark with them are spared to give assurance to those who hear the story that God will not made an end of creation. Toward the end of the story God declares (to God's own self!) that creation will be sustained:

As long as the earth endures,
seedtime and harvest, cold and heat,
summer and winter, day and night,
shall not cease. (Genesis 8:22)

One breathes a sigh of relief. Existential anxiety has at least been assuaged. The central theme of the story is that, in spite of human sin, failure, and finitude, what God has made continues to be. The fear of extinction, and not the problem of human sin, is at the heart of the biblical story of the flood as it is in flood stories from many other cultures.

Like other flood stories, the biblical story of the flood has a happy ending. Within a temporal reality, however, it may well be that not all is well that ends well. Hidden deeply in the story we discover an assuaged but not eliminated anxiety over the potential end of existence. The unsettling phrase, "as long as the earth endures," implies the possibility that in time, the earth may cease to endure. The biblical story provides only temporary relief from the threat, not a permanent solution. Anxiety remains, but it is tempered by faith engendered through the story—faith in the God who brought Noah, his family, and the living creatures through the flood to safety.

Christian Narratives of a Great Fire

In the stories of humankind, great fires as well as great floods bring about destruction both proximately and ultimately. Stories of destruction by flood and fire followed by restoration are widespread across time and cultures.[5] Such stories bravely front the possibility of extinction while harboring a fervent hope for continuation.

A classic example of how the religious imagination plays with the theme of destruction by fire and the possibility of escape is found in *The Pilgrim's Progress* by John Bunyan, an English preacher (1628–1688).

The story begins when the protagonist, Christian, has a strange dream. Waking up from sleep, he was terribly disturbed and returned home to share the dream with his family:

> O my dear wife and you, the children of my bowels, I, your dear friend am in myself undone, by reason of a burden that lieth hard upon me; moreover, I am for certain informed that this our city will be *burned with fire from heaven*, in which fearful overthrow of myself, with

thee, my wife, and you, my sweet babes, shall miserably come to ruin; except (the which, yet I see not) *some way of escape* can be found, whereby we may be delivered.[6]

"Fire from heaven" is a typical religious description of the end of the world, as well as a typical religious metaphor for those more proximate destructions of cities and civilizations that history is replete with. The biblical story of Sodom and Gomorrah is a case in point. As the storyteller relates it, "The Lord rained on Sodom and Gomorrah sulfur and fire from the Lord out of heaven; and the Lord overthrew those cities, and all the Plain, and all the inhabitants of the cities, and what grew on the ground" (Genesis 19:24–25). The devastation was almost total. "All life has been silenced. There is only death—and hopelessness."[7]

This notion of the end of things by fire is not foreign to the New Testament either. It is, in fact, a regular characteristic of what is known as "apocalyptic" literature, religious writings foretelling the end of the world. The apocalyptic Book of Revelation, the last book of the New Testament, said to depict the end time, is filled with images of destruction that stagger the imagination. Among them one finds: "The first angel blew his trumpet and there came hail and fire . . . and they were hurled to the earth" (Revelation 8:7). Fire and a return to existential anxiety! Who could confront the possibility of such destruction with equanimity?

It is, of course, not only human life that it is threatened; the cosmos itself faces destruction. For in those days, "The sun will be darkened, and the moon will not give its light, and the stars will be falling from heaven, and the powers in the heavens will be shaken" (Mark 13:24–25). Anxiety over the threat to personal, tribal, and cosmic existence seems deeply rooted in the human psyche, as evidenced by both the memorializing of ancient cataclysms in myths of destruction and restoration, and by apocalyptic literature.

All of which raises an interesting question. Are these apocalyptic stories, which project the threat of cataclysmic destruction and the possibility of complete extinction into an indeterminate future, any different from the flood stories which memorialize past events of destruction and restoration? As far as the New Testament is concerned, the answer is no. Stories of both past catastrophe and future apocalypse function to generate hope in renewal and continuation in the midst of an experience of existential threat.

Restoration Following the Apocalypse

The Book of Revelation, which brings the New Testament to a close with descriptions of apocalyptic destruction, is not about final endings. It is about proximate endings and a new beginning, a new history, both for humanity and for the entire creation. In sweeping broad strokes, the Book of Revelation paints a picture, not of ultimate destruction, but of continuing creation:

> Then I saw a new heaven and a new earth; for the first heaven and the first earth had passed away, and the sea was no more. And I saw the holy city, the new Jerusalem, coming down out of heaven from God, prepared as a bride adorned for her husband And I heard a loud voice from the throne saying, "See, the home of God is among mortals. He will dwell with them; they will be his peoples, and God himself will be with them; he will wipe every tear from their eyes. Death will be no more; mourning and crying and pain will be no more, for the first things have passed away." And the one who was seated on the throne said, "See, I am making all things new." (Revelation 21:1–5)

It is with this vision of a new beginning, not a final ending, that faith informs present life. The terrifying catastrophe will be over, and order will be restored. The dark night will be gone, and the bright dawn will appear. Despair turns into hope, and death is defeated by life. In short, the entire creation will be renewed and continue its journey into God's future, and we who are given to view the present time, in the light of the eternal within time, are able to live in hope not fear. Why? Because we have faith/trust that the God who stood in the beginning, and spoke creation into existence, stands in the apocalyptic future "making all things new." In faith and in life, we are engaged with the God of the beginning and not the God of the end; with the God of first things and not the God of last things. "In the beginning, God. . . ." Always.

Last Moments, Not Last Things

Contrary to the pronouncements of apocalyptic preachers and literalist believers, there is no such thing as "last things," happenings that mark the absolute end of the world. There are, however, "last moments" in each life, in history, and even in creation. Each moment in time is a last moment. It comes and will not return. Each moment yields to the next moment. We need only observe our own experience. Feelings, sensations, thoughts arise, persist for a while, and pass away, replaced by new feelings, sensations, and thoughts. People come into our lives and leave, and new relationships are formed and lost and formed. Events happen, and then they are over, and something else happens. Nations rise and nations fall. Flood and fire come, and the land is renewed. The cycle of the seasons repeats itself. Every moment is a last moment, but not *the last moment.*

The stories we have briefly considered suggest that each present moment is experienced within an eternal progression of divine creation, which is to say that the temporal and transient exist within the purview of the eternal and therein is our hope. We have our endings, but they are ours, not God's. What God does is to take our endings and make them God's beginnings. The stories want to assure us that endings always yield to beginnings because God is present in all beginnings and endings. "See, the home of God is among mortals. He will dwell with them . . ." (Revelation 21:3).

In our experience of temporality, we have no choice but to face the end of things, including the end of the self and all that the self stands for. In God's eternity, however, we continuously stand at the threshold of the beginning of the self and all that it stands for. God's eternity redeems our temporal experience and fulfills it. In short, we live within God's eternity in time.

Some questions are suggested by these reflections:

1. In what ways are you aware of, and how do you cope with, the existential anxiety expressed in catastrophe narratives and apocalyptic narratives?

2. What would be the psychological consequences of accepting the idea that there are no "last things," only last moments leading to new moments in a continuous movement of divine creation?

3. It what way might such an idea lead to either ethical relativism or ethical seriousness?

4. How might the idea that God is present in all our beginnings and endings affect our reading of Jesus' teaching?

5. How might it affect our understanding of the passion narratives and resurrection narratives?

2. Did Jesus Rise from the Dead and Does It Matter?

The assertion of Jesus' resurrection lies at the heart of Christian faith and thought. The resurrection of Christ has been seen as critical in securing the promise of life after death for believers and, in the more expansive, cosmic vision held by some, for all of humankind. The crucial nature of faith in the reality of Jesus' resurrection is argued most persuasively by the Apostle Paul:

> If Christ has not been raised, your faith is futile and you are still in your sins. Then those also who have died in Christ have perished. If for this life only we have hoped in Christ, we are of all people most to be pitied. But in fact Christ has been raised from the dead, the first fruits of those who have died. (1 Corinthians 15:17–20)

Narratives of the Resurrection

It could be argued that since the earliest days, the real, bodily resurrection of Jesus of Nazareth, murdered by the Romans and buried in a borrowed tomb, has been the linchpin of Christian faith and thought. This raises the question as to what we actually know about the resurrection and gives us pause to wonder if the resurrection is the correct cornerstone upon which to build a life of faith. To enter these questions, we will listen to the accounts of what happened at the tomb of Jesus on the "third day." Mark is the earliest of the canonical gospels; John is the last. Their "resurrection" narratives present some interesting insights into the mind(s) of the early church. We shall begin with Mark.

The "Resurrection" Narrative from Mark

First, however, we should note that the following discussion assumes, along with most biblical scholars, that the Gospel of Mark ends abruptly at chapter 16:8. Both the so-called "shorter ending" of Mark and the so-called "longer ending" were written by some one(s) other than Mark and added to the Gospel, probably in the second century.[8] Why is this important? Because if the Gospel ends at 16:8, then there are no post-resurrection appearances of Jesus in Mark, only the suggestion that such appearances are a possibility; and whether or not there is any expression of faith in the resurrection in Mark is, at best, ambiguous.

According to the Gospel of Mark, "When the Sabbath was over, Mary Magdalene and Mary, the mother of James and Salome, bought spices so that they might go and anoint him [Jesus]. And very early on the first day of the week, when the sun had risen, they went to the tomb" (Mark 16:1–2). The two Marys, followers of Jesus, went to the tomb expecting to find a body. They had watched him die, had witnessed him being taken from the cross, had seen him laid in a tomb, and had seen the tomb sealed. The story makes it clear that they did not go to the tomb expecting a resurrection. Resurrection was something beyond their experience (as it is beyond ours), but not death. They knew about death, had seen it before, had done what was necessary and called for. They would do it again now with the dead body of their beloved teacher.

As Mark fashions it, it is a drama with three distinct moments. First the women are worried as they walk to the tomb, wondering who would role the heavy stone away from the tomb's entrance so they could enter and tend to Jesus' body. In this first moment, there is no expectation that the tomb will be open. It is a moment of grief, not anticipation.

In the second moment, they arrive at the tomb and are disturbed to find it open. They enter, and a young man in a white robe greets them. Is he an angel? Or is he indeed a "young man," perhaps a metaphor for those baptized into Christ's death and resurrection, an image inserted into the narrative by Mark for catechetical purposes some four decades after the accounts narrated? Be that as it may, the women are "alarmed" when they do not find the body, and they do not seem to make the mental leap to resurrection. It is a moment of confusion and growing fear.

In the third moment, "They went out and fled from the tomb, for terror and amazement had seized them; and they said nothing to anyone, for they were afraid." The Greek word translated by the NRSV as "amazement" is *ekstasis*, which can mean either simple astonishment, ecstasy, or a trance like state, or an excess of fear. The context suggests the latter. But of what where they afraid? Had they had an experience of what Rudolf Otto called the *numinous*, the *mysterium tremendum et fascinans*, the mystery that at once produces both awe and fascination, a sense of both dread and attraction?

Other Encounters with the Numinous

A brief look at other biblical accounts of encounters with the *numinous* will raise the possibility that the women's experience at the tomb had as much, if not more, to do with ordinary fear than with an encounter with divine mystery. In the stories of both Jacob and Moses, and in the story of Jesus' transfiguration, we find initial fear/dread in the presence of something extraordinary that transcends rational expectation and explanation, but in each case such fear is accompanied by awe/attraction.

In the story of Jacob (Genesis 28:10ff.), we are told that in a "deserted place," he lay down to sleep and had a dream. In the dream he saw angels ascending and descending upon a ladder that stretched from earth to heaven, and then he heard God transferring to him the promises made to his grandparents, Abraham and Sarah, that is, the promise of land and the promise that he would become a great nation in whom "all the families of the earth shall be blessed" (cf. Genesis 12:1–3).

When Jacob awoke from the dream, "he was afraid," but his next response was to declare, "How awesome is this place." Terror and attraction. Instead of fleeing, Jacob set up an altar to God and named the place Bethel, declaring, "This is none other than the house of God, and this is the gate of heaven."

Like Jacob, the women in Mark's Gospel are afraid of what they encounter in the tomb, but they do not seem to be attracted to it. Awe seems to be lacking; they flee in terror.

Moses also had an experience that transcended rational expectation and explanation but rather than fleeing, he too responded with both awe and fear, attraction and dread (Exodus 3:1ff.). He encounters a burning bush that blazes without being consumed. He is told (senses?) that he is on holy ground and takes off his shoes. He is in the presence of the *mysterium tremendum et fascinans;* he is afraid, but he does not flee. He stays and is commissioned to rescue the Hebrew people from slavery.

Like Moses, the women in Mark's Gospel are given a commission, but they fled and "said nothing to anyone for they were afraid." Again, attraction to the mystery does not seem to overcome the experience of dread.

When Jesus was transfigured on the mountain, Peter, James, and John were present (Mark 9:2ff.). It is another unexpected, non-rational experience, and we are told that the disciples "did not know what to say, for they were terrified." And yet they did not flee; they remained in the experience on the mountain and then descended in the continuing presence of Jesus. They experienced fear and awe but remained in the presence of Jesus. The women in Mark's Gospel, however, seem not to have sensed the continuing presence of Jesus. If anything, perhaps it was the sense of his absence, his death, and the threat his death held for them that terrified them and sent them fleeing from the tomb.

Perhaps the story of the young man dressed in a white robe who told the women not to be afraid, who told them that Jesus had been raised, who told them to tell the disciples that Jesus was going ahead of them to Galilee where they would meet him, perhaps this story, resonating with the early community's faith in the resurrection of Jesus, was read back into an original, starkly frightening memory of an empty tomb. The terrified women's response to the "good news" they "heard" in the story, as Mark tells it, certainly suggests the possibility. Perhaps we have a hard time entertaining that possibility because we read the text with the same faith in the resurrection that enlivened Mark's community.

Had the women had an experience of the divine in the tomb, had they "heard" of Jesus' resurrection, we would expect a different response. Fear yes, but awe as well. A flight from the tomb yes, but in joy not terror, and certainly not in silence. We would expect them to run to the grieving disciples to share this extraordinary "good news."

It was an act of great courage for the two Marys to go to Jesus' tomb to anoint his body. They had witnessed his death, had seen him buried, and knew all about the political, economic, and religious forces arrayed against him. He was murdered because he appeared to be a threat to more than one established order. It is easy to imagine that they would have been afraid that the forces arrayed against Jesus would seek to eliminate his followers as well. It is easy to imagine their fear that attempting to anoint Jesus' body with oils and spices for burial would draw attention to themselves. Was this not the fear that preoccupied them as they started out for the tomb? Did they not harbor this fear when they worried about the very large stone that blocked the entrance to the tomb? When they reached the tomb and found the stone rolled away and the tomb empty, might they not have concluded that the enemies of Jesus had struck again and were waiting in the wings to strike them? Might that explain the fact that they ran from the tomb in terror and in silence? As Mark tells the story, might the empty tomb be a sign of the craftiness of the forces of evil in continuing to work against Jesus and his followers rather than a "proof" of the resurrection?

The "Resurrection" Narrative from John

The account in John's Gospel seems to confirm the worst fears of the women in Mark's Gospel. According to John, Mary Magdalene came to the tomb alone and seeing the stone had been removed from the entrance to the tomb, hurried away and told Peter and "the disciple Jesus loved" that, "They have taken away the Lord out of the tomb, and we do not know where they have laid him" (John 20:2). In this opening scene, there is no trace of the faith of the later church that Jesus had been raised from the dead. Is there, instead, the trace of an original memory of the disciples' suspicion that the grave has been robbed, a common crime of the time?[2]

Mary Magdalene's story is briefly interrupted by an account of how Peter and the disciple Jesus loved went into the tomb and did not find the body of Jesus. We are not told how Peter reacted to the scene inside the tomb; however, we are told that the other disciple entered the tomb, "saw and believed" (20:8). What did he see and what did he believe? We don't know, but John explains, ambiguously to be sure, "for as yet they did not understand the scripture, that he [Jesus] must rise from the dead" (20:9). Could it be that he saw the grave cloths, as Peter did, in the empty tomb and "believed," as Mary did, that the body had been stolen? This brief interlude in Mary's story ends with the observation that, "Then the disciples returned to their homes" (20:10). Would we not have expected a much more dramatic response from them if either of them had seen the empty tomb and "believed" in a resurrection.

When the two disciples departed, Mary was left alone with her suspicion, a suspicion that increased her desolation. She had not only lost her beloved teacher but also been deprived of the last privilege of serving him by properly preparing his body for burial. According to John's telling of the story:

> Mary stood weeping outside the tomb. As she wept, she bent over to look into the tomb, and she saw two angels in white sitting where the body of Jesus had been lying, one at the head and the other at the feet. They said to her, "Woman, why are you weeping?" (20:11–13)

Curiously, Mary tells them what she had earlier told to Peter and the other disciple, "They have taken away my Lord, and I do not know where they have laid him" (20:13). Without a word in response, the angels leave the story, and Mary is left with the conviction that Jesus is dead, his body stolen. Unless you are reading into the story what is not yet there, there is no hint up to this point of resurrection. Of course, the story does not end here. Mary is still at the tomb.

Suddenly, she sees a man standing there. It is Jesus; however, Mary does not recognize him; rather, she takes him for the gardener. He asks why she is weeping, and for the third time she responds out of the conviction that his body has been stolen: "Sir, if you have carried him away, tell me where you have laid him, and I will take him away" (20:15).

The meaning of the story, up to this point, is that for Mary, Jesus is dead. Her weeping is not a sign of faithlessness. Quite to the contrary, her very presence at the tomb is a sign of her continuing faithfulness, and her weeping is a testimony to her deep love for her dead teacher and friend. The story, to this point, has the ring of truth to it. The remainder of the story is a reading into the narrative by the storyteller of the faith held by the church some sixty years later.

The "risen" Jesus addresses Mary Magdalene by name, and she responds by calling him "Rabbouni," which means teacher. She has recognized him in the speaking of her name (in the mutuality of love?). John then inserts a brief aside on the theme of Jesus' ascension, and Mary Magdalene hurries away in joy to announce to the disciples that she has seen the Lord (20:18).

What is John's point in crafting a story that centers on the fact of Jesus' death rather than faith in his resurrection? Might he not have a catechetical reason? Could he not be suggesting to the community of faith for whom he was writing that while "resurrection" is an enigma best left within the mystery of God, the experience of an "appearance" of Jesus, the experience of a continuing sense of Jesus' presence both personally and in the community, is grounded in unassailable devotion and love for Jesus, like Mary's?

Before moving on to consider further the notion of "appearances" of Jesus, let's reflect on a few questions suggested by Mark and John:

1. What, if any, impact might it have on the life of faith to view these stories as appearance stories rather than resurrection stories?

2. Why is it (or is it not) helpful to recognize the catechetical function of the canonical gospels?

3. What questions might catechumens have been asking that encouraged Mark and John to tell these post-crucifixion stories as they did?

4. In what way might such questions be (or not be) relevant to new Christians in the twenty-first century, and are these stories helpful (or not) in addressing such questions in our context?

We now turn to other implications for the life of faith of stressing the motif of appearance rather than resurrection. As we shall see, this is not to deny the resurrection, but it is to distinguish between faith and experience. No one witnessed the resurrection of Jesus; it is thus a matter of *faith* inferred from the *experience* of a continuing sense of Jesus' presence among and within the faithful.

Post-Crucifixion Appearances of Jesus and Transformation

We have seen that neither Mark nor John give us a resurrection story; rather, John gives us an "appearance" story, and Mark points to the hope of a later appearance. Does this mean that Jesus is not risen? Possibly, but not necessarily. Post-crucifixion experiences of Jesus' appearance and continued presence in the community of faith may well imply resurrection, but they do not require a resurrection. Although no one saw Jesus rise from the dead and could thus "prove" the resurrection, the early church came to a strong, vibrant faith in the resurrection, a faith that has persisted to this day. This faith was derived—and I would argue, continues to be derived—from the experience that this Jesus, who was dead, is now alive and with us and within us. It is this experience that grounds Christian life and faith and not the "fact" of the resurrection.

The appearances of the crucified Jesus to his followers dramatically changed their relationship to him and to his message. The frightened and dispirited disciples were inspirited and emboldened to live "in Christ" and proclaim his message "in Jerusalem, in all Judea and Samaria, and to the ends of the earth" (Acts 1:8). In the words of Luke, the author of Acts, they had received "power" from the Holy Spirit, which they came to understand as the Spirit of Christ (cf. 2 Corinthians 2:17).

This power has proven more powerful than all the powers and principalities of the world put together. It is rooted in the faith that Jesus is not dead, but living, not just living, but living powerfully to transform women and men into his "image" and inspire them for the work of God's kingdom (cf. 2 Corinthians 2:18). The logic of the early church seems to be that if Jesus "appears" to his followers then he is living, and if living, then he has a continuing claim on them. If Jesus is actively engaging his followers to carry on his work, then he has been raised from the dead. The appearance stories come to be told and heard as resurrection stories. The empty tomb has come to stand for the victory of the power of life over the power of death.

It is this Jesus, experienced to be present and believed to be risen, who *appeared* to Saul in a visionary experience of such power and persuasiveness that he was converted from a persecutor of the Church to a tireless evangelist for Jesus' cause.

Now as he was going along and approaching Damascus, suddenly a light from heaven flashed against him. He fell to the ground and heard a voice saying to him, "Saul, Saul, why do you persecute me?" He asked, "Who are you, Lord?" The reply came, "I am Jesus, whom you are persecuting. But get up and enter the city, and you will be told what to do." (Acts 9:3–6)

Saul, now known as Paul, makes no claim to an exclusive appearance experience. In his first letter to the Christians in Corinth, Paul reports, as if it were common knowledge that:

[Jesus] appeared to Cephas, then to the twelve. Then he appeared to more than five hundred brothers and sisters at one time, most of whom are still alive, though some are dead. Then he appeared to James, then to all the apostles. Last of all, as to one untimely born, he appeared also to me. (1 Corinthians 15:5–8)

Although there are no resurrection stories, per se, there are many other appearance stories in the New Testament. Though they may differ as to details, the common theme running through them all is the sudden awareness that Jesus who was dead and buried is now present, and this living presence of Jesus is transformative. It also appears that in most (though not all; remember Paul) the causative factor in the appearance is the mutuality of love between the follower of Jesus and Jesus. The last appearance to Peter in the Gospel of John is instructive.

Jesus, who at his last meal with his disciples, expressed the depths of his (and God's) love for them, appears to Peter following the crucifixion. Peter, out of fear for his own safety, had denied knowing Jesus three times on the night he was betrayed into the hands of the authorities. Now Jesus appears to Peter and asks him—three times—"Peter do you love me," and Peter responds three times, "Lord, you know that I love you." Jesus then commands Peter three times to "Feed [and tend his] sheep." Then, interestingly, Jesus foretells a life of bold faithfulness in following him for this man who had so recently denied him. The pattern seems clear: love, appearance, power, transformation.

Appearance stories such as these are the true cornerstone upon which Christian faith, thought, and practice has been built. Which is to say that Christian faith is experientially grounded. Because appearance narratives appear to reflect inner, visionary, or contemplative experiences, it is easy to see how they not only gave rise to resurrection narratives, but also to theological formulations such as Paul's confession, "It is no longer I who live, but it is Christ who lives in me" (Galatians 2:20).

We have no experience of the resurrection, but we do experience, both individually and as communities of faith, the continuing and transforming presence of Jesus who once was dead. We can, therefore, leave the enigma of bodily resurrection to the mystery of God and still unequivocally affirm that Jesus rose from the dead and is powerfully living and present with and within us.

And now a few questions to ponder before moving to the next chapter:

1. What, if any, practical significance is there in Paul's claim that Jesus appeared to hundreds of Christians, including, presumably, many who did not know him before his crucifixion?

2. What implications might there be for contemporary worship in emphasizing post-crucifixion stories of Jesus as appearance stories rather than resurrection stories?

3. If the impetus for Christian mission is found in the appearance and experience of the living Jesus, from where should the "content" of mission come and what should that "content" be?

4. If Christian faith is, in fact, experientially grounded, what are the implications for faith formation in Christian congregations?

5. How could the apparent biblical pattern of "love, appearance/experience, power, transformation" undergird both individual and communal spirituality?

3. Healed or Saved? Or Both?

There are many questions that confuse and trouble us when it comes to the relationship between religion and health, be it physical health, psychological health, or spiritual health. Is there a relationship between faith and healing? If so, why are some who seem to have faith apparently not healed? And why are there biblical stories of healing without apparent faith?

What are we to make of the fact that the Greek words usually translated as "salvation" and "to be saved" can also be translated as "healing" and "to be healed or restored to health"? Are we to understand this in ultimate terms or can it also be understood in penultimate terms? In the same light, what are we to make of the fact that the Greek word usually translated as "to heal a physical ailment" can also be translated as "to heal spiritually" and "to restore from a state of sin"? Are health, wholeness, and well-being comprehended by the term salvation; and if so, does not salvation have to do with this life as well as life after life?

Existential Anxiety and the Felt Need to Be Healed and Saved

If there is anything that all of humankind are aware of (dimly aware of at some times, intensely aware of at others) it is the fact of finitude and mortality, biological fragility, and death. We talked earlier of the existential anxiety that goes with the human condition, as we live precariously from birth toward death, an anxiety that is often heightened in times of serious illness or accident and always heightened when the diagnosis is of a "terminal condition." Most humans, to one degree or another depending on current circumstances, feel a dual necessity—the proximate need to be healed and the ultimate need to be saved from extinction.

For healing of the body and mind, most people go to the medical professionals, chief priests in the domain of physical and mental healing. For salvation from extinction, people either live in denial of death, face the music and accept extinction as reality, or go to the religious professionals, chief priests of salvation. Indeed, it is not too much to say that for many if not most religious people, eternal life is the goal, and thus the meaning, of the present life.

Many, if not most, religious believers pursue religious activities because they offer them the promise of eternal life. Without being cynical, I believe it is fair to say that much of the worship and acts of piety religious believers engage in are motivated, in good part, by existential anxiety and the desire to be saved. This is true not only of the Christian religion. To one degree or another, in one way or another, the destiny of the self, what happens when the individual dies, is an important concern in most religions.

Whether in Hinduism (where the goal of religious practice is experiential realization of the truth that *atman*, or individual soul, is one with *Brahman*, or universal Soul), or in Buddhism (where realization of the impermanence of the self leads to the experience of no-self and enlightenment), or in Christianity (where the resurrection of the dead into an eternal relationship with God is promised), religion is concerned with the ultimate destiny of the self-conscious self. Most religions tend to approach their adherents with both a "carrot and a stick" to encourage them to follow "appropriate" religious practices. The carrot is the promise of "salvation," however construed, while the stick is the threat of unpleasant consequences, for example, a chain of transmigrations and reincarnations in the case of Hinduism and Buddhism and judgment and damnation in the case of Christianity.

Be that as it may, what most religions have in common is that they primarily (particularly in their popular forms) understand "salvation" as an end of life concern, and therefore, there is a practical tendency to separate concerns about health and concerns about salvation with health taking second place to salvation in terms of importance. Health is seen as a material concern, a physiological and psychological concern. Salvation, on the other hand, is a "spiritual" concern. Health is a "here and now" concern; whereas salvation is a "then and there" concern, and then and there matters most.

This does not seem to be the way Jesus understood things. From what we can know about him in the Gospels of the New Testament, he appears to have been as interested in this life as much if not more than he was in the next life. He thought not so much in terms of "eternal life" as he did in terms of the kingdom or rule of God, a kingdom that he saw breaking into the world, not least of all, in his acts of healing.

Jesus, the Healer of the Body and the Soul

In Christian faith and thought that take seriously the teaching and practice of Jesus of Nazareth, the material and the spiritual, health and salvation, cannot be so easily divorced. Indeed, they coalesce. The notion of salvation does not belong to the after-life alone; it has to do with this life as well. We should not forget Jesus' claim that he came so that we might have life and have it abundantly (John 10:10). Health and well-being are important for the experience of an abundant life and that people experience such a life mattered to Jesus because he believed it mattered to God.

Most Christians revere Jesus as the savior. His death on the cross "for us" is seen as redemptive, as having the intention and power to bring about salvation/redemption. The blood Jesus shed on the cross is said to wash and purify those who believe, enabling them to enter God's eternal life. Trusting in the saving power of Jesus' sacrifice, we approach death in the confidence that we are "saved." In this understanding, salvation is fundamentally a matter of the soul and the after-life. Salvation is out there, ahead of us, which serves to minimize and relativize the significance of life in this world.

But did Jesus think about, teach, and practice salvation in the same way as his later followers, or did he see salvation as a function of the present unfolding of the rule of God? Did he see salvation as a matter of the body as well as of the soul, as a matter of wholeness and wellbeing, and is that why healing figured so prominently in what he did and in what he instructed his disciples to do?

A look at the way Christology (doctrine of Christ) and soteriology (doctrine of salvation) developed in the early centuries of the church leads one to suspect that Jesus' later followers were far more under the influence of both the Jewish understanding of sacrificial atonement through the shedding of blood and Greek philosophical dualism with its denigration of the body than Jesus was.

Narratives of Healing Apart from Faith

Many stories in the Gospels show Jesus as a very effective healer, effective to the point that the crowds would not leave him alone. Mark reports that:

A great multitude from Galilee followed him; hearing all
that he was doing, they came to him in great numbers
from Judea, Jerusalem, Idumea, beyond the Jordan, and
the region around Tyre and Sidon. He told his disciples
to have a boat ready for him because of the crowd, so
that they would not crush him; for he had cured many,
so that all who had diseases pressed upon him to touch
him."(Mark 3:7-10)

It appears that it was his fame as a healer more than
his fame as a preacher that "spread throughout all Syria,
[so that] they brought to him all the sick, those who were
afflicted with various diseases and pains, demoniacs, epi-
leptics, and paralytics." (Matthew 4:24)

We should note that in these and in parallel accounts
there is neither mention of faith nor reference to God. What
takes place seems to be no more than physical healing which
Jesus apparently values in and of itself as a sign of the rule of
God. If there is faith in these accounts, it is the faith of the
healer, Jesus' faith in God and in the rule of God.

When Mark tells us that people came to Jesus from
"beyond the Jordan, and from Tyre and Sidon," he is telling us that many of the people who came to Jesus were
Gentiles, non-Jews who did not share Jewish faith. We can
assume that the crowd from these gentile regions "sought
Jesus because of his healings, not to submit themselves to
the reign of God."[1]

Why did Jesus heal them? They did not share his faith
in the God of Judaism, nor did they observe the religious
laws, rituals, and customs of the Jews. Jesus must have
been aware that they did not come to hear his message of
God's rule, and he apparently did not see them as potential converts to his faith in God as the loving Father. He
saw them simply as people afflicted with physical and
mental ailments who longed to have their health restored,

and he believed that mattered to God. Should he reject them because they were not from his ethnic and religious background? Should he refuse to heal them because they were only seeking physical well-being and not spiritual well-being? Or did thoughts such as these cross his mind at all? Jew or Gentile, what motivated Jesus to heal seemed to be his compassion for those who suffered and his desire to relieve that suffering. More than once the Gospels tell us that, "When . . . he saw a great crowd . . . he had compassion for them and cured their sick" (Matthew 14:14).

We are simply told that "power came from him [Jesus], and [he] healed all of them" (Luke 6:19). No question was asked of them and no demand made of them. He had the power to heal, and he healed them. The implication is clear. Jesus understood restoring people to health and well-being as an integral part God's rule and therefore of his ministry. Grounded in Jesus' (God's) compassion, healing was unconditional. He certainly did not see it as a means to bring about a change of religious commitment. He healed because people were sick in body or mind or spirit.

That Jesus understood healing as essential to the rule of God, which he proclaimed, is evident in his reply to John the Baptist who was in prison and sent his disciples to ask Jesus whether he is "the one who is to come," that is, the one who is to inaugurate the rule of God. This is Jesus' reply: "Go and tell John what you hear and see: the blind receive their sight, the lame walk, the lepers are cleansed, the deaf hear, the dead are raised, and the poor have good news brought to them. And blessed is anyone who takes no offense at me" (Matthew 11:2–6). Although many who would like to "spiritualize" the rule of God do take offense at him, such things are the stuff of the kingdom of God. The material has a spiritual dimension. Indeed, for Jesus it appears that the distinction between the material and the spiritual, the secular and the sacred, is a false distinction.

The Healing of a Leper

A story of the healing of a leper, with parallels in all three synoptic gospels, makes the point that healing has psychological, social, and spiritual dimensions as well as a physiological dimension. According to Luke 5:12–13:

> Once, when [Jesus] was in one of the cities, there was a man covered with leprosy. When he saw Jesus, he bowed with his face to the ground and begged him, "Lord, if you choose, you can make me clean." Then Jesus stretched out his hand, touched him, and said, "I do choose. Be made clean." Immediately the leprosy left him.

When the leper "bowed with his face to the ground," it was an act of humility and supplication, not an act of worship. His request demonstrated a remarkable confidence in Jesus as a healer. Here again the reputation of Jesus as a healer is implied, and we can suspect that if the leper had faith, it was in Jesus as a healer and not in Jesus as either Son of God or Messiah.

What is extraordinary in this story is that in all three versions, Jesus touches the leper to heal him. Mark adds the detail that he was "moved with pity" (Mark 1:41), another indication that Jesus' healing was motivated by compassion for those who suffer, irrespective of their faith commitments. This story presents a vivid picture of how Jesus' acts of healing involve far more than the alleviation of physical ailments. The interrelationship of the physical, the psychological, social, and spiritual dimensions of life is dramatized by Jesus' compassionate touch. One wonders how long it had been since this man had felt a human touch; how long since he had been included in family and social life; how long since he had felt included rather than excluded from the circle of God's people. According to Leviticus 13:45–46:

The person who has the leprous disease shall wear torn
clothes and let the hair of his head be disheveled; and he
shall cover his upper lip and cry out, "Unclean, unclean."
He shall remain unclean as long as he has the disease;
he is unclean. He shall live alone; his dwelling shall be
outside the camp.

How long do you have to cry out "Unclean, unclean"
before you internalize the message and believe that it is true
of your whole being? There is no doubt that the leper in
this story felt cut off not only from family and community,
but from God. When Jesus touched him he (1) healed him
physically, (2) ended his familial and communal exclusion
and isolation, and (3) demonstrated to him that he was not
outside the circle of God's people/love. Here is the "good
news" that accompanied Jesus' healing, the all inclusive love
of God for the "least of these." For the leper, healing and
salvation coalesced in Jesus' touch.

Without downplaying Jesus' concern for the eternal life,
we must insist on his equal, if not greater concern for this life
and the way people experience this life. How else to understand his overriding concern with the social, political, and
economic dimensions of God's rule? If, as Christians have
long maintained, salvation has to do with ultimate deliverance from the "powers and principalities" and entrance into
the presence of God, it seems clear that Jesus understood that
within the limits of finitude, deliverance and relationship
with the divine can be experienced in the here and now.

In Jesus' so-called high priestly prayer in John 17:3, he
declares that, "This is eternal life, that they may *know you,
the only true God, and Jesus Christ* whom you have sent"
(emphasis added). Not later, now! Could we not say that it
was the knowledge of God through the touch of Jesus that
the leper experienced? Which is to say, again, that healing
and salvation coalesce in Jesus' touch. Healing is a proximate experience of ultimate salvation.

The narratives suggest that Jesus healed people who did not share either his faith in God or in the rule of God. They also suggest that he understood healing as an experience of the rule of God, irrespective of who was healed. Physiological, psychological, and spiritual ailments are symptomatic of a world needing deliverance in the here and now from the "principalities and powers" that bedevil human life, robbing it of well-being. Jesus apparently understood his healings of Jew and Gentile alike, as an assault on those powers and principalities and thus, as acts of deliverance/salvation. All of which raises some interesting questions to ponder before moving on to consider the relationship between faith and healing.

1. If healing in its broadest sense includes personal, interpersonal, communal/societal, and spiritual healing, what are the implications for the mission and ministry of the church?

2. How would affirming healing (in both the narrow and broad sense) as both a sign of and an experience of the rule of God impact ethics?

3. What are the implications for both Christian ministry and Christian involvement in interfaith relationships of Jesus' apparent willingness to heal people irrespective of their religious faith?

4. How would affirming healing as an act of "deliverance and relationship with the divine" affect the way we think about Christ, salvation, and the church?

Narratives of the Relationship
between Faith and Healing

Although the canonical gospels make it clear that in many
healing stories it is the faith of Jesus and not the faith of the
one healed that is sufficient for healing, there are many other
stories where the faith of individuals and, on occasion the
community itself, is involved in the healing process. In all
these stories, faith is seen as a necessary condition for healing, be it the faith of the healer, the faith of the one healed,
the faith of the community, or all working together.

A Paralytic Is Forgiven and Walks

Mark 2:1–12, and its parallels in Matthew and Luke, provide
us with a highly dramatic healing story in which the faith of
several people plays a critical role. A paralyzed man is carried
by his friends to the place Jesus is teaching, presumably about
the rule of God. They cannot reach Jesus due to the crowd
and so they climb to the roof above the room where Jesus sits,
break open a hole, and lower their friend into Jesus' presence.

One can imagine the surprise, commotion, and annoy-
ance of those intently listening to Jesus' teaching. As for
Jesus, we are only told that he "saw their faith" (2:5). The
plural pronoun implies that what he saw was the faith of
both the paralytic and those who carried him to Jesus. We
have here an interesting depiction of the communal dimensions of faith. Could we not say that it is the common faith
and compassion of these men (and perhaps women) that
provided the context for healing?

Christian tradition has held that faith is an essential element of salvation, as is the prevenient forgiveness
of God. Both elements are present in this story, and both
also appear to be essential to the healing that takes place.
After acknowledging the faith of the paralytic and those

who brought him to him, Jesus said to the paralytic, "Son, your sins are forgiven" (2:5). Jesus is immediately criticized for this and accused of blasphemy. It is, after all, only God who can forgive sins. To demonstrate that he is acting on authority from God, and as an instance of the rule of God, he orders the paralytic to "stand up, take your mat and go to your home" (2:11). To have faith is to become aware of forgiveness, which is to be saved, which is to be healed. The physical and the spiritual are integrated in Jesus' healing act.

Faith is clearly central to this story. The faith *of the healer* in the authority, compassion, and power of God; the motivating faith *of the community* in the healer, and the personal faith *of the one who experiences healing and salvation* in the healer. In this story it is likely that the healing was an illustration of what Jesus had been teaching at the time he was interrupted. That being the case, one can imagine that faith in Jesus as more than a healer was awakened among those in the crowd. One suspects that he was beginning to be perceived as the bringer of what he proclaimed—the rule of God. Be that as it may, this story gives us a window on one important aspect of life under the rule of God—health and wholeness of people matter.

A Woman's Faith Leads to Healing

The story of a woman who suffered from hemorrhages for twelve years is another example of the coalescence of faith, healing, and salvation (Mark 5:24–34). Mark sets the stage for this dramatic healing by noting that "a large crowd followed him [Jesus] and pressed in on him" (5:24). In the crowd was a woman who desperately desired to have her chronic disease healed. She stealthily came up from behind Jesus and touched his clothes. "If I but touch his cloak," she said to herself, "I will be made well" (5:28). And touch she did. The effect was instantaneous. "Immediately," the story tells us, "her hemorrhages stopped, and she felt in her body that she was healed of her disease" (5:29). As to Jesus, even though he seemed totally unaware of what was going on, he felt that "the power had gone forth from him" (5:30).

What healed the woman? Jesus did not touch her; he did not even see her. Even though he was "immediately aware that power had gone forth from him," he apparently did not know to whom that power had gone and what that power had done. What else could his statement, "Who touched my clothes?" mean (5:30)? When the woman identified herself, "in fear and trembling" (for she had broken a whole host of social and religious taboos), and told Jesus what she had done and what had happened to her, he declared, "Daughter, your faith has made you well ("saved you" in other translations); go in peace, and be healed of your disease" (5:34).

Mark seems to be saying that the healing/saving energies/power of God are in Jesus, and faith gives one access to that power. It was the woman's faith, not Jesus' conscious intention, that drew the healing/saving power of God to her.

When Faith Meets Faith

Mark 9:14–29, the story of the healing/exorcism of a spirit-possessed boy (epileptic?), encourages us to think more deeply about the role of faith in healing/salvation; however, before we examine the story itself, a few preliminary considerations are in order. The first attempt at healing in the story, which fails, is carried out by the disciples in Jesus' absence. The story immediately preceding this healing attempt explains Jesus' absence. It is the story of the transfiguration—a story that some scholars have suggested might be an appearance/resurrection story read back into the narrative of Jesus' earthly ministry.[2] Were that to be the case, this healing/exorcism story would appear to be a catechetical set piece crafted to teach Mark's audience the way the community of faith accesses the healing power of God in Jesus' (physical) absence. To anticipate the conclusion, what is required is (1) prayer and (2) the meeting of faith with faith.

While Jesus is on the "Mount of Transfiguration" with Peter, James, and John, a distraught father brings his spirit-possessed son to the remaining disciples. From the story we know that he is looking for Jesus but, not finding him, in his desperation he asks the disciples to heal his son. They make an attempt and fail. Jesus returns. The father explains his son's illness and the disciples failure to heal him. Jesus chastises everyone present as a "faithless generation." The father apparently confirms Jesus' judgment by pleading with him: "If you are able to do anything, have pity on us and help us" (9:22). Jesus responds sharply, "If you are able!—All things can be done for the one who believes" (9:23). What is it that the father has failed to believe? The power of Jesus to heal? The consistency of compassion in the rule of God? Both?

Is it too much to suggest that we hear the echo of an earnest seeker's plea in the father's plaintive confession: "I believe; help my unbelief!" Apparently that confession is enough for an experience of the compassion and healing power of Jesus—the spirit is cast out, the boy is healed of his affliction.

The story turns to the would-be healers (the community of faith?). They ask Jesus, "Why could we not cast it out?" His answer is profoundly instructive: "This kind can come out only through prayer" (some ancient authorities add *and fasting*) (9:28–29).

If this is indeed a catechetical set piece, then Mark is highlighting four realities of the rule of God for the community of faith: (1) healing is an act of God; (2) faith opens one to the healing energies/power of God, and thus faith establishes a context for healing/salvation to take place;

(3) faith is nourished and strengthened through the many forms of prayer (and the disciplines of the spiritual life?); and (4) healing in the church is a matter of faith meeting faith, the faith of the healer meeting the faith of the one seeking healing (cf. James 5:13–16).

Faith as Openness to the Divine

Modern medical researchers are learning what people of faith have always known—there is a positive relationship between faith and health and general well-being. Although science will probably never discover the "mechanism" that drives this relationship, there seems to be a growing body of evidence supporting it. Be that as it may, faith is neither panacea nor placebo.

In generic terms, faith is openness to something greater than oneself, to a loving, compassionate power with the will to heal (in its broadest sense) and to save. In Christian terms, faith is openness to the God that Jesus disclosed and to the rule of God that Jesus proclaimed, a kingdom of God within which health and well-being are intrinsic values. In the openness of faith, the healing/saving energies of God are released both within and through individuals in ways we may not be able to explain, but which have been and continue to be experienced by the faithful.

Because Christian faith is faith in the God disclosed in the life, teaching, death, and post-crucifixion appearances of Jesus, and because Christian faith is an expression of motivating trust in the rule of God that Jesus proclaimed, the desire for health and well-being cannot be divorced from the values of the kingdom that support health and well-being—notably, justice and loving kindness. Justice and loving kindness are the defining characteristics of faith in the God of Jesus.

Physical Body – Spiritual Body

Before leaving our consideration of faith and healing, perhaps a final word about mortality is in order. Christians pray for healing—which they must do if they have faith in and are open to the God disclosed by Jesus; however, such prayer must be done with an awareness of the limitations of finite, biological existence. Even those who experience healing will one day die. Faith cannot prevent biological death. The human mortality rate is 100 percent, which is to say that prayer for *physical* healing will for all of us one day be ineffective.

This is not, however, an impediment to the life of faith. If anyone was aware of mortality and its implications for the life of faith, it was Paul. He seemed to understand that our finite and thus limited experiences of healing/salvation prefigure the complete healing/salvation that will be experienced when the "spiritual body" replaces the physical body in the resurrection. In 1 Corinthians 15:42–44, Paul writes:

> So it is with the resurrection of the dead. What is sown is perishable, what is raised is imperishable. It is sown in dishonor, it is raised in glory. It is sown in weakness, it is raised in power. It is sown a physical body, it is raised a spiritual body. If there is a physical body, there is also a spiritual body.

Faith in complete healing and complete salvation with the resurrection of the dead sets the context within which Christians pray for finite healing and work together to create a social, political, economic, and religious environment based on the values of the rule of God that support health and well-being for all.

A few questions before moving on to consider the relationship between Christianity and the other great religions of the world:

1. What might be the theological and pastoral concerns in asserting that faith and forgiveness are necessary conditions of healing?

2. What might be the potential impact, both positive and negative, on personal devotion and communal worship if faith and forgiveness were stressed as central elements in healing?

3. How could the communal dimension of faith be used to create a congregational environment where healing seems plausible? Would that be a good idea, and why or why not?

4. In what way might the assertion that, generically construed, faith is openness to the divine, to a loving, compassionate power with the will to heal, provide a starting point for ecumenical interfaith conversation and cooperation?

5. Does the affirmation that incidents of healing are temporal experiences of salvation coupled with Paul's notion of the "spiritual body" help to alleviate the existential anxiety that accompanies illness, injury, and the prospect of death? Why or why not?

4. All Roads Lead to Rome?

The expression "All roads lead to Rome" has been used, often by those of a skeptical if not cynical nature, to suggest that irrespective of what religious path one takes, all religious people will ultimately arrive at the same destination. At some levels, perhaps, but at other levels it does not seem to be the case. It all hinges on how one defines "Rome."

Defining "Rome"

The well-known historian of religion, Mircia Eliade, has provocatively observed that, "Salvation is but another name for religion. That is, all religions are basically conceived as means of saving people at one level or another. And there are always two aspects to religion: what people are to be saved *from* and what people are to be saved *to*."[1] One could argue from this statement that religion is not so much a matter of doctrine as it is a matter of life. As we noted in the previous chapter, Jesus' religious commitments moved him to a ministry of saving people *from* physical, mental, and spiritual sickness *to* physical, mental, and spiritual well-being *in this life*. We suggested that Jesus' healing was an act of deliverance or salvation.

If "saving people at one level or another" is the heart of most religions, one would expect a fundamental accord among religions, mutual respect, and an eagerness to work together in the cause of salvation "at one level or another." But this is not the case. The history of the relationship between religions is filled not with accord, respect, and cooperation but with discord, disdain, and division. How is this to be explained? What causes religions to be suspicious of, if not hostile to, each other?

Let me suggest that the answer might lie in the mutually exclusive doctrinal systems, concepts, and interpretive language/categories that the different religions employ—and insist upon—in attempting to make absolute claims about truth and salvation. At the level of salvation where salvation is understood as a "life after life" concern, if one stays within the doctrinal systems, concepts, and interpretative tools of a particular religion, and if one insists that only they are valid, then all religious roads do not, and perhaps cannot, lead to Rome.

Does this condemn us to live in a religiously divided world? Perhaps, and then again, perhaps not. It depends on whether or not we can "bracket" our differences long enough to shift our focus from the level of absolute claims to truth to the level of life concerns, from salvation principally understood as a life after life issue to salvation disclosed in daily experiences of deliverance in this life from whatever impedes genuine human well-being. That is, if we can define "Rome" in terms of such everyday experiences of deliverance, we may well find that all roads do, indeed, lead to Rome and in fact, converge long before Rome is reached. We may also discover that, regardless of which religion we adhere to, we are journeying to Rome surrounded with wonderfully interesting and insightful traveling companions.

What, after all, is most important, abstract doctrinal systems that are concerned with the next life or a practical spirituality that values this life? If our interfaith conversation and cooperation is focused on the level of this-worldly deliverance from the "powers and principalities" that diminish, damage, or destroy life, then we have things to say to each other and learn from each other. Hearing from people of different contexts, cultures, and religions about how they understand, experience and confront the "powers and principalities" can be very enlightening. And on this level it is reasonable to expect that the spiritual insights and ethical demands of the various traditions will inform and enlarge each other.

The Blind Men and the Elephant

A well known Buddhist parable can illustrate the need to refocus our attention from the level of ultimate salvation to the level of everyday experiences of deliverance. The parable recounts how a group of the Buddha's disciples, who were in a village to beg alms for the day, encountered several religious sectarians who were also begging alms and quarreling while they did so. They were men of diverse views, diverse aims, and diverse opinions, all of which were grounded in diverse faiths and diverse "truth" claims. They were quarrelsome and abusive with each other and generally obnoxious and annoying to those around them.

When the Buddha's disciples returned, they told him about the sectarians and their behavior. The Buddha responded by observing that, "These sectarians, Brethren, are blind and unseeing. They know not the real, they know not the unreal; they know not the truth, they know not the untruth. In such a state of ignorance do they dispute and quarrel as you describe."

He then went on to tell a story about several blind men who encountered an elephant. Some of the blind men who felt only the elephants head declared confidently that the elephant was a large pot. Those who examined the ears said with equal confidence that the elephant was a winnowing basket. Those who felt the tusk said the elephant was a plowshare, while those who felt only the legs said it was a pillar. And so it went. They soon fell to quarrelling, shouting,

"Yes, it is!" "No, it isn't!" "An elephant is not that!" "Yes, it is that." Eventually they took to attacking and hitting each other.

When the Buddha finished his parable, he told his followers, "Just so are these sectarians who are wanderers, blind, unseeing, knowing not the truth, but each maintaining it is thus and thus."[2]

If we take the elephant as a metaphor for the absolute and/or ultimate salvation and the blind folks as a metaphor for the various religions of the world, the point is clear. No one fully apprehends the absolute. What we apprehend is, at best, partial and limited. While the various religions may each hold some truth, none of them has the whole Truth. That is an inescapable fact of finitude.

As long as the man clinging to the elephant's leg insists that the leg is the whole of the elephant, his believing and thinking will go places that the faith and thought of the fellow holding on to an ear cannot go, and they will have little to agree upon and less to cooperate in. In this sense, when it comes to the nature of the absolute and salvation, all roads do not, and perhaps cannot, lead to Rome. Although what each of the world's religions claim to be true about ultimate realities may be a part of such realities, the conclusions they draw from what they hold to be true are wrong because they assume that their partial apprehension of ultimate realities is in fact the ultimate reality itself. Here is the root of sectarian intolerance and evangelical arrogance.

Religion as a Way of Life

So how can the religions of the world choose a destination that they can get to together and also discover each other as good traveling companions? I suggested earlier that if we agree to bracket absolute claims and focus our common attention on everyday issues and concerns, it may be possible to find a destination all roads can lead to. By "bracket" I do not mean to ignore or diminish the value of any religion's insights into the absolute; I mean we should set them aside in our interfaith conversation and cooperation. Remember the observation of Eliade, which I noted in the opening of this chapter, that "all religions are basically conceived as means of saving people *at one level or another.*" If we leave our beliefs and practices regarding ultimate things in our churches, synagogues, mosques, and temples, we might more readily share with each other our beliefs and practices on things that have to do with our everyday lives, and we might also more readily work together outside of those holy places from a common commitment to life.

I am suggesting that the commitment to fullness of life for all people can be a spiritual meeting ground for people with different beliefs in ultimate realities. For this to happen, however, religious adherents need to recognize the sacredness of everyday life and need to see that religion is not so much a way of thinking as it is a way of living. This may be easier in the East than it is in the West.

In the West, one finds a tendency to distinguish the "religious" from the remainder of human life. A line is drawn between the secular and the sacred. Generally speaking, whereas the home and the holy place are accepted as the sphere of religion, the marketplace, the world of politics and commerce, the institutions of government and economics are decidedly not the sphere of religion. When religion is separated from the every day concerns of human life it becomes preoccupied with clerical hierarchies, correct teachings, official doctrines, formalized creeds, and so on. Whether or not these teachings, doctrines, and creeds have anything to do with the actualities of the life we live in the world is generally not a primary concern. As to whether they can be, or even should be, translated into ethical action becomes secondary to whether or not they are "believed."

Religious ethics are reduced to private as opposed to public morality.

In the East, however, there is a tendency to see what is "religious" as closely related to all aspects of human life, to the point where being religious is understood as a way of life. From public religious worship to private religious devotion; from religious festivals marking rites of passage such as birth, marriage, and death; to the veneration of ancestral spirits; from religious sacrifices to dedication of a new house or a new business—human life is religious. In the East, to one degree or another, religion continues to affect almost all aspects of life.

In the world outside the West, to live is to be religious and to be religious is to live. Note that I am using the adjective "religious" and not the noun "religion." To be religious is not primarily to subscribe to a set of creeds and doctrines, but to live life in awareness of the presence of the spiritual world and to make efforts to fulfill the ethical expectations of the religious community to which you belong.

C. K. Yang, in his study of religion in Chinese society, defines religion as the "system of beliefs, ritualistic practices, and organizational relationships designed to deal with critical matters of human life such as the tragedy of death, unjustifiable sufferings, unaccountable frustrations, uncontrollable hostilities that threaten to shatter human social ties."[3] Although Yang's definition does not extend to critical matters on the brighter side of life where religion also has an important role to play, for example, the raising of families, earning a living, and contributing to the welfare of the community, he does make it clear that religion is about this life. Religion, Yang argues, helps people address these critical events which are an inherent part of life. Religion enables people to find "strength from faith in such non-empirical realms as spiritual power inspired by human conceptions of the supernatural."[4]

Religion, in other words, cannot be reduced to a system of "correct" teachings, creeds, and doctrines about the absolute and/or concerns about the next life. Religion must be "this worldly," in the sense that it provides resources for addressing the questions and problems experienced in this life. Religion, viewed in this way, is more of an emotional, ethical, and spiritual undertaking than a speculative and intellectual enterprise. It is more a matter of the heart than a matter of the head, more a matter of devotion to divine realities and commitment to responsibilities of life, than a matter of assent to doctrinal affirmations and agreement on theological formulations.

Religion then, as has been suggested, is "a form of life that seems to those who inhabit it to be comprehensive, incapable of abandonment, and of central importance."[5] In short, religion is a way of life. In this respect, it is interesting to note that, according to the book of Acts, in the earliest days of the Jesus movement, this new faith was not called Christianity, it was called "the Way." The *Didache*, a first century Christian manual of instruction, begins by noting that "There are two ways, one of life and one of death, but a great difference between the two ways. The Way of life, then, is this: First, you shall love God who made you; second, love your neighbor as yourself. . . ."[6]

Religion as a way of integrating the spiritual and the material in everyday life is, on the whole, how believers of different religions understand their faith in Asia. This is true for Christians in Asia as well. Living in the midst of other religions, Christians are rediscovering the importance of some passages in the Bible that they have tended to neglect, passages that insist upon the spiritual and ethical dimensions of everyday life, for example, 1 John 4:20: "Those who say, 'I love God,' and hate their brothers or sisters, are liars; for those who do not love a brother or sister whom they have seen, cannot love God whom they have not seen."

Living among believers of other faiths, who practice their religion as a way of life, also prompts Christians to take a second look at what the Apostle Paul said to the Christians at Rome: that is to say, "A person is justified by faith apart from works" (Romans 3:28). As we all know, this verse was singled out by the Reformers of the sixteenth century as pivotal in understanding the gospel; however, the man who wrote that we are justified by faith apart from works also wrote that, "the only thing that counts is faith working through love" (Galatians 5:6). The Spirit is not manifested by intellectual assent to doctrinal truth, rather it is manifested in "love, joy, peace, patience, kindness, generosity, faithfulness, gentleness, and self-control" (Galatians 5:22–23b).

Religion as a way of life is not an inflexible script that dictates behavior and robs people of the freedom to make their own moral choices. Quite to the contrary: a continually changing context requires a continual reexamination of our moral choices. We live in a world of constant change, development, and technological innovation, and so we face questions and issues that would never have occurred to either our ancestors or the founders of the various great religions. Religion as a way of life simply argues that the spiritual and ethical insights of the many religions in the world can be, and must be, resourced in addressing the changing realities of the world we live in.

Let's stop for a moment and consider some questions suggested by what we have discussed so far:

1. From the church's point of view, what would it mean to stress religion as an ethical and spiritual "way of life," rather than primarily as a system of beliefs, doctrines, creeds, and so on, safeguarded by a clerical hierarchy?

2. How might catechetical instruction change if we affirmed that faith is not primarily a way of thinking or

a way of believing, but rather is a way of life grounded in particular ways of thinking and believing about the absolute (God)?

3. In this world of increasing inter-religious misunderstanding, mistrust, and violence, in what ways might shifting the focus from "God" and the next life to the spiritual and ethical dimensions of this life help religions find common ground for conversation and cooperation?

4. What might the "content" of this common ground be?

5. Do you agree that our finitude requires both humility and openness in the relationship between religions? If so, how might such humility and openness manifest themselves?

The Wrong Way and the Right Way

Perhaps a look at two different ways of "being religious" will highlight the importance of understanding religion in terms of the practice of compassion rather than as assent to doctrine. Religion understood as assent to doctrine, in a very real sense, dehumanizes individuals by considering them outside the context of their individual lives. They are all too easily reduced to statistics. Religion understood as the spiritual practice of compassion, however, apprehends the unconditional value of all human beings and affirms that value in a practical commitment to justice and loving kindness.

Pope John Paul II and the Wrong Way

In what turned out to be a sadly controversial visit by Pope John Paul II to Asia in November 1999, we have an unhappy confirmation of the fact that all roads do not lead to Rome when religious systems of belief and doctrine and the hierarchical structures of religious power are emphasized at the expense of others. The continent of Asia houses three-fourths of the world's population, and less than three percent of the Asian population are Roman Catholic believers. India, the world's second most populous country, is a Hindu nation. Out of its almost one billion people, 83 percent are Hindu, 11 percent Muslim, 2 percent Christian, 2 percent Sikh, and 2 percent of other religious faiths. In this religiously diverse but heavily Hindu nation, the Pope issued a proclamation in which he made the following declarations:

1. "There can be no true evangelization without the explicit proclamation of Jesus as Lord."

2. "The peoples of Asia need Jesus Christ and his Gospel."

3. "Asia is thirsting for the living water that Jesus alone can give."

4. "Just as in the first millennium the cross was planted on the soil of Europe, and in the second on that of the Americas and Africa, we can pray that in the third millennium a great harvest of faith will be reaped on this vast and vital continent."[7]

In this Hindu nation, the Pope emphasized that the only true evangelization is that which "explicitly" refers to Jesus as Lord. Although the Pope may have been simply pointing to the centrality of Jesus in Christian faith, the non-Christian audience of the Pope's declaration heard the word *evangelization* as *proselytization,* as an inducement to leave false faiths for the true faith.

By arguing that Asia thirsts for what Jesus "alone" can give, he again devalued the faith and experience of non-Christian people. The assertion that Jesus "alone" can provide what people need seems a bit like holding on to the leg of an elephant and declaring that the leg is the whole of the elephant. That little word *alone* excludes all other realities and possibilities in matters of faith and salvation. Would Jesus make such a claim for himself were he to come to Asia today? I suspect not, but the Pope had no trouble making it on his behalf and in doing so, greatly diminished the possibility of genuine conversation and cooperation between faiths on matters crucial to the well-being of non-Christians and Christians alike.

When the Pope envisioned "a great harvest of faith" in Asia in the third millennium, he again marginalized and devalued the faith that was already in Asia and at the same time polarized Christianity and other religions in ways that easily lead to mutual mistrust and religious violence. At a gathering in India of representatives of several religions, the Pope said that, "Religious freedom constitutes the very heart of human rights. Its inviolability is such that individuals must be recognized as having the right even to change their religion, if their conscience so demands."[8] One suspects that he was implicitly defending the "right" of Christians to proselytize and the "right" of Hindus, Moslems, Buddhists, and others to become converted to Christian faith. Conversion, of course, is primarily understood as assenting to the truth claims of the new religion while rejecting those of the old religion and has little, if anything, to do with a heightened commitment to justice and loving kindness in the way the convert lives his or her life.

Jesus and the Right Way

Religion as Jesus understood it, experienced it, and taught it is an example of what C. K. Yang described as "diffused religion."[9] Diffused religion does not live principally in "holy

places," where it is enshrined and codified; rather, it is diffused in the relationships, institutions, and moral choices
that make up the lives of faithful people. For Jesus, faith
could never be reduced to intellectual assent to a creed;
rather, faith was a living out of one's trust in God through
all the vicissitudes of life. Diffused religions tend to be religions of the people rather than religions of a clerical hierarchy, and they tend to have the power to bring people closer
together as they seek spiritual and physical/psychological
well-being in the midst of the uncertainties of life. Which is
to say that the notion of diffused religions might give us a
more constructive approach to the reality of religious pluralism. It encourages us to meet as spiritual people on the
common ground of the common good while abandoning
the attempt to convert each other to allegedly absolute and
mutually exclusive "truths."

The gospel accounts indicate that Jesus looked at human
need and responded to it. He gave priority to life over religious law as evidenced in his healing on the Sabbath and his
assertion, when criticized for it, that the Sabbath was made
for people and not people for the Sabbath. Jesus taught the
rule of God, which he understood as the rule of love and
justice, the rule of compassion and mercy. In his understanding of religion, the rule of God is not something to be
codified and enshrined and paid lip service to—it is to be
lived.

Jesus' approach to the life of faith is perhaps best expressed
in the Prophet Micah's declaration that what God wants from
us is nothing more, and certainly nothing less, than that we
do justice, love kindness, and walk humbly with our God
(Micah 6:8). Such religion "diffuses" the rule of God into all
of the relationships and structures of human life in such a
way as to enhance human well-being. It precludes discrimi-
nation based on religion, race, class, gender, or anything else.
Jesus calls upon people of whatever background to tend to

the fundamental business of life, which is caring for life. This call of Jesus to care for life is the primary Christian voice in inter-faith conversation and cooperation.

A Spiritual World

What emerges from Jesus' ministry of God's rule is the vision of a spiritual world in which humanity is engaged in the quest for wholeness of life, a quest guided and enriched by the consciousness of God present in people's daily lives. In this spiritual world, our dependence on one another for the protection and enrichment of life is expressed in the ethical imperatives of love and justice. No religious tradition can claim a monopoly with respect to these impera- tives. All religious traditions have something to learn from all other traditions with respect to these imperatives.

What ultimately matters is the priority of life with both its vulnerabilities and expectations for wholeness. The pri- ority of life should displace religious boundaries with the realization that in the face of the vulnerabilities and expec- tations of life, we are all equally vulnerable and hopeful, no matter where our religious loyalty lies. Therein lies the motivation for the religions to journey together toward the common destination of human well-being while enlighten- ing each other with their distinctive spiritual insights into the meaning and value of life.

A middle-aged woman, in a Native American commu- nity in northwestern Alberta, Canada described her people's religious understanding by saying, "The most important thing about our native way is that it is a spiritual way. We are spiritual people. No one can take this spirituality away from us."[10] When we realize that we are spiritual people, shaped by our experience of the divine in the struggle for life and not merely religious people, shaped by our creeds, doctrines, or articles of faith, then we also realize that we live in a spiritual world shared by all beings created by God. Such a realization has the power to move us beyond the parochialism of our religions into serious conversation about what matters—life. The more people of different faiths interact around common issues of life and death, the more insight we all gain into spiritual strategies to confront those issues.

More questions to ponder before moving on:

1. Is proselytization theologically defensible? Why or why not?

2. In what ways, other than through doctrinal confession, might a Christian affirm the centrality of Jesus in his or her spirituality?

3. How might Jesus' teaching on, and practice of, the rule of God be "diffused" in the contemporary social, political, economic, and interfaith context?

4. If the different religions can somehow truly meet on the common ground of the common good, would it be possible for each tradition to get a better sense of the "elephant"? If so, how? If not, why not?

5. How Can We Know God and What God Wants?

For religious people the questions of how we can know and experience God, and how we can know what God wants for us and from us, are matters of perennial concern. If God is the subject of religion, it seems a matter of the first concern to be able to some degree know God and to have confidence that what one knows is God. Apart from that, religion makes no sense at all.

This perennial concern of religious people suggests several questions for us to consider. Can the finite apprehend the infinite? If so, then where and under what conditions? Is God to be known only in scripture, or are there signs of God in nature and history and perhaps even in human creativity? If there is continuing revelation, then how can we have any confidence that what we take to be disclosures of God, in both nature and human events, are in fact disclosures of God and not simply the exercise of either an overactive religious imagination or spiritual wishful thinking? And, if God is also disclosed in scripture, how can such disclosures be a resource for tracing the footsteps of God in the world we inhabit? What about the apparent contradictions in biblical images of God? If we believe that our perceptions of God are in fact real, if limited and partial, how can they gain some measure of credibility in a world of cultural and religious pluralism? Is it possible that experiences of the divine that shape other religious traditions could have genuine revelatory value not only for them but for Christians as well?

The Problem of Revelation

In both the Hebrew and Greek languages, the words we translate as *revelation* carry the meaning of to disclose, to uncover, to unveil, and thus to reveal. The word carries the same meaning in everyday secular usage where we might speak of revelations in the investigation of a crime or a scandal, or when we marvel when the drape cloth is removed to reveal an as yet unseen beautiful painting which in turn reveals an unknown artist's talent. The word *revelation* assumes the hiddenness of what is revealed, something unknown becomes known. That which was hidden is at least to some degree made clear.

In the biblical tradition, God is hidden, veiled, as it were, by transcendence. God is infinite Spirit; humankind is finite flesh and blood. That said, the biblical tradition also affirms that there is a level of correspondence between God, the creator, and humankind, God's creatures, which allows for both divine disclosure and human receptivity to that which is disclosed. In both the Hebrew and Christian scriptures, the spirit of God, "falling upon" or "residing within" human beings enables some degree of human perception of both God and God's will. In the biblical understanding, the divine can be apprehended.

This understanding is experientially grounded in both biblical religion and in other religious traditions. The experience we referred to in chapter 2 as an encounter with the *mysterium tremendum et fascinans*, the mystery that at once produces both awe and fascination, a sense of both dread and attraction, is a panhuman experience and gives us confidence that there is indeed something transcendent to be revealed. It also gives us confidence to expect that the revelation of and receptivity to God's purpose and activity extends to religious traditions other than our own.

The problem, of course, is that revelation is not straight forward. If, as the biblical tradition insists, historical events, personal experiences, prophetic utterances, dreams, visions, and other extraordinary experiences can be revelatory of God and God's will, it must be admitted that the meaning of events and experiences is rarely immediately evident. Interpretation is necessary if their revelatory content is to become clear and efficacious. Which raises the question of credibility. Are there any criteria by which we can determine if any allegedly revelatory word, event, or experience is in fact revelatory? Are there any interpretive categories that can be applied to allegedly revelatory words, events, or experiences to both search out their meaning and then make credible statements to those both within and outside the faith community about that meaning and its implications for personal and communal life?

The Exodus and Jesus' Teaching and Practice of the Rule of God

According to the biblical tradition, the answer to these questions is yes. There are historical events that are so critically formative in the self-understanding of particular religious communities that such events become a lens through which the revelatory content of other events and experiences can be discerned. In the Hebrew experience, the Exodus, the liberation of the Hebrews from slavery in Egypt (and the consequent receiving of the law on Mount Sinai) is one such event. In the Christian experience, the life, teaching, death, and post-crucifixion "appearances" of Jesus in the community form the lens through which Christians continue to discern the presence of the divine in human affairs. If it is consistent with Jesus, it is of God; if it contradicts Jesus, it is not.

The assertion that the tradition provides interpretive categories for tracking the footsteps of God assumes that religion cannot be reduced to a history lesson. It is not so much about what God did as it is about what God is doing. The Exodus event and the giving of the law with their themes of liberation, justice, freedom, covenant, human well-being, and human responsibility provide distinct categories for discerning and interpreting God's presence and activity in the present world of human affairs. As God was, we expect God to be. Jesus' consistent proclamation and practice of the rule of God (even to the point of death) echo and develop the major themes of the Exodus and the Decalogue and provide similar categories for present discernment and interpretation of God's ubiquitous activity in the world.

A summary statement of how both Hebrews and followers of Jesus discerned what is and what is not of God in both human affairs and personal experience can be found in Deuteronomy 30:19–20, where God, speaking through Moses, tells the people of God:

> I call heaven and earth to witness against you today that I have set before you life and death, blessings and curses. Choose life so that you and your descendants may live, loving the LORD your God, obeying him, and holding fast to him; for that means life to you and length of days . . .

The revelatory content of historical events and personal experiences can be discerned by this one question: What in the event or experience is a choosing of life, and what is a choosing of death? As difficult as it may sometimes be to distinguish between the two, God will be found in the former.

Where Was God in the Events of September 11, 2001?

Take as an example the world-shaking events of September 11, 2001. The attacks on the World Trade Center in New York, the Pentagon in Washington, D.C., and the foiled attempt to strike the White House with United Flight 93 are clear examples of a choosing of death, and therefore, they cannot be interpreted as a direct revelation of God or the will of God. Those who argued, and there were many, that the attacks represented God's judgment on America for tolerating homosexuality and abortion were not using the criteria of life to discern God's role. They were projecting their own hatred and propensity for violence onto God (more about this later) and using that as the lens through which they searched for God. Naturally they found what they were looking for.

And when some prominent Christians "blamed Islam itself for the attacks, denouncing the faith of some 1.3 billion Muslims around the world as an evil and wicked religion,"[1] it was another xenophobic choosing of death. The proclamations of these Christians had no revelatory content; God was not in them.

Those who argued, and there were those who did, that the attacks were in some way divine judgment on America's political and economic sins in the global arena were also not using the criteria of life to discern God's role. Such folks have also projected their own hatred and propensity for violence onto God and used it as the lens through which they search for God. One could make a persuasive case on the basis of what the ancient Hebrew prophets taught, not to mention Jesus' proclamation of the rule of God, that God might well unfavorably judge America's way in the world, but it would be a choosing of death, not life, if God would use an act of supreme violence in passing that judgment.

The 9/11 attacks were a choosing of death and thus cannot in themselves be seen as revealing God's nature. But did they provide a revelatory occasion? It is a very different question, and I would argue that the answer is yes. So, what might have been revealed of God's will in that horrendous day of violence? Many things, I suspect, but one interesting suggestion comes from a *Newsweek* article by Kenneth Woodward. In reflecting upon what might come out of the tragedy, he noted that:

> What theologians from various traditions are beginning to realize is that we cannot truly understand the uniqueness of our own tradition unless we also develop a deep understanding and appreciation of at least one other religion. What committed Christians and Jews and Muslims must do is find within their own traditions sound theological reasons for valuing other faiths without compromising the integrity of their own. This is already beginning to happen. Despite some concern from Vatican officials, some prominent Catholic theologians are beginning to ask how the Holy Spirit might be at work within non-Christian religions. Some Muslim scholars, too, are using the Quran to show that religious pluralism has been blessed by Allah himself. Clearly, this will be the most important theological agenda of the new millennium.[2]

Here we can discern a choosing of life in the movement, however tentative, toward mutual understanding and mutual respect, eventually leading, perhaps, to cooperation in other choices for life. When the criteria of life moves Christians to wonder, while the flames of violence are still burning, "how the Holy Spirit might be at work within non-Christian religions," including Islam, our knowledge and experience of God is expanding. If, as we have suggested, the Spirit of God inspires and enables us to perceive what God is doing in the world, it seems that we can discern the footsteps of God in the new questions being asked by both Christian and Islamic thinkers about the relationship between these two great religions.

When Revelation Is Used to Deceive and Manipulate

In hierarchical religious institutions, the clerical class is more often than not, either *de jure* or *de facto*, both the guardians of revelation and the channels of revelation. When revelation is claimed to be the sole prerogative of priests and pastors, rabbis, imams and mullahs, it clearly gives them considerable power and authority over the faithful. Their clerical position is used to give both credibility and coercive power to whatever "revelatory" pronouncements they might make, be they interpretations of their religion's scriptures and traditions or new "revelations" of "God's will" for the present moment.

The fact that the notion of "revelation" can be abused to further a religious or political agenda or ideology will not come as news to anyone. The Hebrew scripture has many instances in its prophetic literature of such deception and manipulation by those who hold positions of religious authority. To give just one example,

Therefore thus says the Lord GOD: Because you have uttered falsehood and envisioned lies, I am against you, says the Lord GOD. My hand will be against the prophets who see false visions and utter lying divinations; they shall not be in the council of my people, nor be enrolled in the register of the house of Israel, nor shall they enter the land of Israel; and you shall know that I am the Lord GOD. Because, in truth, because they have misled

my people, saying, "Peace," when there is no peace. . . .
(Ezekiel 13:8-10, cf. Jeremiah 6:13-14)

It is perhaps not too much to assert that control of
the processes of revelation is critical to sustaining the
power of a clerical hierarchy. Those who apparently control access to the will of God in and for the present have
a powerful tool for controlling the thought, emotion, and
behavior of the faithful. This is not to suggest that all religious leaders as a matter of course abuse their authority
in this way; it is to suggest, however, that it is not uncommon, and that, if the above text is any indication, God
looks dimly upon it.

The contemporary rise of radical fundamentalism in
many religious traditions can, I suspect, be traced in part to
the fierceness with which some leaders defend their authority to discern, interpret, and impose the "revelation" they
have "received," both from the tradition and from their personal "encounter" with the divine. When the meaning of
revelation is narrowed to the point that it serves to promote
the ideological interests and religious assertions of powerful, and thus privileged, religious leaders, what we have is
not genuine revelation; it is a choosing of death.

Social, political, scientific, and technological changes in
the last two centuries have in many denominations greatly
diminished the power of those who control the processes of
revelation and thereby control the faithful. In our eclectic,
complex, interdependent, information-based world, many
religious people claim for themselves the freedom to seek
"revelation." Today many who are not religious professionals seek an understanding and experience of God and the
will of God, through (1) their own interpretation of sacred
texts, (2) their own participation in spiritual disciplines, (3)
their own experiences of something extraordinary, (4) their
own encounter with the wisdom of other traditions, (5)
their personal integration of what science and technology

tell us about both the world and human being, and (6) their own critical social analysis.

The result of all this is a tendency to broaden the range of revelation to include far more than sectarian concerns. Questions of personal and communal well-being, the quest for justice egalitarianism, and freedom from oppression, have for many become proper subjects for revelation in the confidence that God cares about these things as much as— if not more than—God cares about the confessions, theologies, legalisms, rites and rituals, and power structures of sectarian institutions. One cannot help but recall the revelatory voice of Amos 5:21–24:

> I hate, I despise your festivals, and I take no delight in your solemn assemblies. Even though you offer me your burnt offerings and grain offerings, I will not accept them; and the offerings of well-being of your fatted animals I will not look upon. Take away from me the noise of your songs; I will not listen to the melody of your harps. But let justice roll down like waters, and righteousness like an ever-flowing stream.

The potential in this tendency to broaden the range of revelation is a healthy diffusion of religion into social and cultural life with an accompanying decentralization of spiritual life. Spirituality is not limited to what you do in "holy places"; it is what you do wherever you are. Contrary to the thinking of many religious leaders, with the distinction between choosing life and choosing death as a primary criteria for discerning what is and is not a revelation of God's will and activity, the broadening of the range of revelation and the decentralizing of who has access to revelation is not a threat to the rule of God that Jesus proclaimed; it furthers that rule. The "democratization" of the processes of revelation and discernment raises interesting new questions and problems; however, apart from such democratization, religion will be increasingly irrelevant to and isolated from the other domains of life, and religious assertions will command no credibility or conviction outside the religious domain.

Let's stop a moment and consider some questions raised by the previous discussion:

1. What are some examples of how religious leaders have used their control of revelation to control the beliefs, thoughts, and behavior of the faithful?

2. Is the so-called "democratization" of revelation good or bad? Why?

3. What are some potential dangers of democratizing revelation, and how can they be protected against?

4. It what ways might the broadening of the range of revelation to include more than sectarian concerns further the rule of God proclaimed and practiced by Jesus?

5. Do you agree that the distinction between choosing life and choosing death provides an interpretive tool for attempting to discern what might be revelatory in historical events and personal experience? Why or why not?

6. What are the theological and ecclesiastical implications of affirming that the search for revelation is more than historical study of ancient texts?

What Do I Encounter, God or Me?

The story of Jacob's dream, which we considered in chapter 2, interestingly raises another concern that we need to address with respect to revelation. When Jacob was fleeing his brother, Esau, whom he had cheated of his birthright and from whom he had stolen their father's blessing, he lay down to sleep in the wilderness, exhausted and feeling both helpless and hopeless. As he slept, he had a dream in which he saw angels ascending and descending on a ladder that stretched from earth to heaven. In the dream, God spoke to him and assured him that the fulfillment of the promises given to Abraham and Sarah would be continued in him. Those promises were that God would create a nation from them and their descendents that would be both divinely blessed and an agent of blessing to the other nations. Note that the revelatory content of the dream had to do with God's choosing life and entrusting the choosing of life to Jacob and his descendents.

When Jacob awoke, he recognized his dream as an encounter with the divine, and he was both awe-stricken and afraid. "Surely the Lord is in this place," he concluded, "and I did not know it" (Genesis 28:16). He called the place "Bethel," the house of God, and set up a stone there as both symbol and reminder of the revelation. It is important to note that the content of this very personal revelation is taken as a revelation of God precisely because it resonates with the community's previous understanding of God's will and action in the affairs of the community. God is a God who chooses, promises, blesses, and commissions his people for the sake of all life. One expects consistency from God. Recall Paul's admonition to the Christians in Corinth who were arguing over revelation that, "the spirits of prophets are subject to the prophets, for God is a God not of disorder but of peace" (1 Corinthians 14:28).

The story of Jacob's dream raises two important questions. (1) Did he actually encounter the divine in his dream or only the product of an overly active religious imagination? (2) What do you do when supposed revelation reveals contradictory images of God? The questions are related.

Ludwig Feuerbach and Psychological Projection

In an important book called *The Essence of Christianity*, the nineteenth century German philosopher, Ludwig Feuerbach, argued that God is a human construction, a fiction taken for a fact. According to Feuerbach, the worship of God is nothing more than the worship of an idealized self. Humans, he maintained, idealize their own best (and sometimes worst) attributes and then externalize them by projecting them onto "God."

The psychology of projection is well known, and we all do it. It seems easier both to hate ourselves and to love ourselves in others than it is in ourselves, and so we project what we don't like or do like about ourselves onto others, with the result that we relate to our projections rather than to the individuals we saddle with them. I suspect, as Feuerbach did, that the same mechanism is at work in our relationship with "God." Much, if not most, of what we believe to be true of God is a projection of human attributes and aspirations. We have, in other words, created God in our own image and this, conveniently it must be said, secures divine sanction for our own agendas, ideologies, and behaviors.

The point to be made, however, is that the psychology of projection does not mean that there is no real entity upon which I place my projections. When I project what I like or don't like, desire or don't desire onto a spouse, a child, a friend, or a colleague, it doesn't mean that there is no a real person behind my projections, one who bears little resemblance to my projections, one who I don't really know precisely because of my projections.

Here is where we part company with Feuerbach. God is not a fiction. Just because the God we "know" and "worship" is largely a creation of human projection does not mean that there is no God behind the projection, a God we do not really know, and who most likely bears little resemblance to our projections. As it is with people, so it is with God. By recognizing and detaching from our projections, the "other" is revealed, unveiled, uncovered, known.

This is not a new idea. Luther spoke of the "hidden God" and the "revealed God," and it is easy to argue that Jesus' teaching and practice function to help us recognize and detach from the projections that have created the conventional images of God that hide God. To the degree that we are able to recognize and detach from our projections, we are open to the experience of revelation.

Is there a transcendent being behind human projections and consequent images of God? Was there an objective referent to Jacob's supposed experience of the divine? Who knows? There certainly can be no "proof" one way or the other; however, millennia of human encounters with something extraordinary and spiritual both suggest that there is such a reality. Faith in a God discovered in the human apprehension of a spiritual dimension to reality led the biblical tradition to affirm, as we noted in the beginning of this chapter, that there is a level of correspondence between the subject of that perception (God) and humankind.

Contradictory Images of God

Even a quick reading of the Hebrew Scriptures and the New Testament will reveal a wide range of images of God, many of which contradict each other. This is particularly true when we compare images of God as a deity who uses extreme violence to accomplish divine purposes with images which stress the divine forbearance and divine commitment to justice and loving-kindness. It is difficult to reconcile the two.

If the image of God as one who employs merciless violence in accomplishing divine purposes is affirmed, then those who saw the events of 9/11 as divine judgment against America for tolerating homosexuality and abortion would be right to claim that the attacks of 9/11 were revelatory in themselves. The killing itself would have told us something about God.

With what we have said about projection and with what we know about the human proclivity to violence, it seems reasonable, however, to suspect that images of God as a wrathful, violent, and vengeful deity represent the projection of our own violence upon God in order to gain divine sanction for that violence. That would be just as true in the New Testament as it is in the Hebrew scriptures. This of course leaves us with two choices. We can either rationalize the irreconcilable differences in such images of God, or we must *choose* which image of God we will take as revelatory, recognizing, of course, that such choosing is an act of faith.

It seems to me that those whose faith places them under the rule of God proclaimed by Jesus and grounded in his consciousness of God, must choose images of God that support the choosing of life, not the choosing of death. Those images then become the lens through which we discern what is and what is not of God when we read scripture and the living documents of contemporary events and personal experience. That being said, we should recall Thomas Merton's suggestion that we never underestimate our ability to deceive ourselves and acknowledge that in a finite, sinful, and thus morally ambiguous world, it is quite often extraordinarily difficult to discern the difference between choosing life or death, those things that make for genuine human well-being and those things that do not.

Jesus the Revealer and the Rule of God

The Christian doctrine of incarnation, the notion that the *numinous* was somehow embodied in Jesus of Nazareth, gives Jesus, for Christians, pride of place as *the* lens through which we look in attempting to discern both the truth about God in scripture and the presence and will of God in contemporary events and experience. In the confessional, metaphorical language of John 1:14, in Jesus, "the Word became flesh and lived among us." John also has Jesus declare to his followers, "Whoever has seen me has seen the Father" (John 14:9). Paul makes the same point when he states that, "For it is the God who said, "Let light shine out of darkness," who has shone in our hearts to give the light of the knowledge of the glory of God in the face of Jesus Christ" (2 Corinthians 4:6).

Unfortunately, under the historically understandable but perhaps regrettable influence of the Reformation, it is common to believe that what Jesus mostly revealed about God was his will to save humankind through the free gift of salvation in an eternal life that begins at death. Without gainsaying the importance of such a "revelation," it seems that is not principally what Jesus thought his life and teaching was about. According to the Gospel of Luke, Jesus understood his "unveiling" or disclosure of God in very different terms:

He stood up to read, and the scroll of the prophet Isaiah was given to him. He unrolled the scroll and found the place where it was written: "The Spirit of the Lord is upon me, because he has anointed me to bring good news to the poor. He has sent me to proclaim release to the captives and recovery of sight to the blind, to let the oppressed go free, to proclaim the year of the Lord's favor." And he rolled up the scroll, gave it back to the attendant, and sat down. The eyes of all in the synagogue were fixed on him. Then he began to say to them, "Today this scripture has been fulfilled in your hearing. (Luke 4:16–21)

This passage, of course, can be spiritualized and given a next life orientation; however, if Luke can be believed, that's not what Jesus did. As we have already seen, the rule of God in the here and now was the primary orientation of Jesus' life and teaching. Understood this way, the text provides a critical perspective for "finding" God both in scripture and in life.

In another interesting text in Luke, Jesus locates the rule of God firmly in this life:

Once Jesus was asked by the Pharisees when the king-dom of God was coming, and he answered, "The king-dom of God is not coming with things that can be observed; nor will they say, 'Look, here it is!' or 'There it is!' For, in fact, the kingdom of God is among you [within you]." (Luke 17:19–20)

One concludes, therefore, that understanding Jesus' teaching and practice of the rule or kingdom of God is determinative for Christians attempting to discern the lineaments of the kingdom in the events of human life. It is the calling of those who follow Jesus to recognize the rule of God and make it real in the world. The pattern observed above, in our consideration of Jacob's encounter with God, continues in the experience of Christians: God chooses, promises, blesses, and commissions for the sake of life.

Now for a few questions before moving on:

1. In a world where more and more ordinary people seek to discern and interpret for themselves the activity and purposes of God, what is the role of the pastor or other religious leaders with respect to revelation?

2. What is the role of the community of faith in the discernment and interpretation of revelation?

3. What images of God can you find in the Bible and which of them still play an important role in the way people think about and "experience" God?

4. Why is it (or is it not) important which images of God take pride of place in both public worship and private devotion?

5. What difficulties might we encounter in attempting to distinguish between choosing life and choosing death in making ethical decisions?

6. What Is the Church?

When talking about the church, it is good to realize that unless we are talking about a specific denomination, almost everything we say is by necessity a generalization. Keep that in mind as we move through this chapter. Throughout Latin America, Africa, Asia, and North America, there are hundreds upon hundreds of conservative evangelical and Pentecostal churches, as well as a multitude of expressions of the so-called mainline churches.

When talking about the malaise of the church, most of my comments will be reflective of the mainline churches, but when talking about the character of the church, much of what I say will be addressed to churches across the ecclesiastical spectrum, even those that appear to be booming. Membership is not always the best indicator of the degree of a church's faithfulness to the rule of God proclaimed by Jesus. Look, for example, at the burgeoning churches in the United States that proclaim a gospel of prosperity that sanctions cultural and economic values and practices that Jesus would most likely look askance at.

Be that as it may, it is clear that many Christians, as well as non-Christians, today are disillusioned or worse by the church. Church demographics, particularly but not exclusively of mainline denominations, indicate that more people are leaving the church than entering the church. Major mainline denominations such as the United Methodist Church and the Presbyterian Church USA report major net losses in church membership each year. Although many who leave mainline congregations migrate to more experientially focused churches such as those of Pentecostal or so-called neo-Pentecostal (Charismatic) persuasion, many others gravitate toward New Age movements or Eastern religions to find ways to understand and express their spirituality. Others simply drop out of organized religion entirely in favor of either personal and private spirituality or adopt secular alternatives to religion as a way to find meaning and direction for their lives. In short, large segments of the church seem to have lost—or be losing—their ability to provide relevant spiritual direction and life meaning to people who feel the need for it.

Many Christians apparently no longer find the dogmas, rites, and rituals of the church that once nourished them with the hope of heaven meaningful any longer or relevant for the lives they live from day to day. Many of them, in spite of once active participation in the worship, educational, and service life of the church, slip out the back door of mainline churches and are never seen again. For many of them, it seems that the hope of heaven is no longer a sufficient reason to affiliate with a church. They are not looking for the gateway to heaven as much as they are looking for an experience of the life of the spirit in the here and now—one which helps to make sense of the here and now.

I mentioned that the church is in trouble not only with Christians but with non-Christians as well. Both the adherents of other religious faiths and those of a thoroughly secular persuasion seem to find the church's teaching irrelevant to life's major issues, at best, and appalling in its practice, at worst. Scandals involving church leadership, the perception of hypocrisy, internecine hostility, pretensions of superiority vis-à-vis other religions, right-wing Christians pressing wedge issues into ideological political agendas, left-wing Christians' equally ideological and ineffectual liberal posturing in political and economic spheres, all this and more cause many to miss the message and so dismiss the church as an irrelevant social, cultural, and religious entity in the course of contemporary human affairs.

Should we be pessimistic? I think not. There are clearly grounds for concern that should stir people of Christian faith to analysis and action, and we should never assume that the demise of any particular institutional expression of Christian faith is the demise of Christian faith itself. This world is God's creation and as Luke noted in Acts 14:17, God has not left himself without a witness anywhere. Neither God nor the human experience of God are threatened if particular denominations leave the stage of history. Spiritual experience, as we have noted, is deeply rooted in humankind, and there is no reason to think that the religious impulse is endangered when particular religious institutions are endangered. Those who care about particular religious institutions, however, need to see contemporary trends as a serious wake-up call.

In his study of Christianity in Asia, the historian, Samuel Moffett, noted what should be the obvious: "Christians have always been their own worst enemies. In the final analysis, the deadliest obstacle to any community of Christians is to be found not outside it but within it."[1] To look outside of Christian communities of faith to find the reasons for the malaise of the church is a futile exercise. The answers to the malaise and apathy of the church are to be found within.

The Ethos and Ethics of the Church in the World

To say that this is a critical juncture in the history of Christianity would not be an overstatement; however, one suspects that there are few if any moments in the history of Christianity that have not been critical points in time. As a very human, and thus finite and limited institution, the church must always be questioning whether or not it is

correctly discerning and following the will of the God who
has called it into existence for divine purposes.

Cosmetic changes will not do. The church that lives by
the slogan, the technique, or the latest fad will die by the slogan, technique, and latest fad. When Jesus called the community of those who follow him the "salt of the earth," "a city
set on a hill," and the "light of the world" (Matthew 5:13–14),
he was not throwing slogans around. He was pointing to the
community of faith as integral to the life and well-being of
the world when it internalizes and lives by the rule of God in
full view of the larger public community. To take Marshall
McLuhan's famous expression out of context, "the medium
is the message." As the church is, so is its message.

It is not uncommon to hear talk about the nature of the
church, the essence of the church, the mission of the church.
Such expressions tend toward the abstract and thus do not
speak clearly to people looking for more practical reasons
for affiliating with the church as a venue for spiritual experience. I am suggesting, therefore, that we speak of the "ethos
and ethics" of the church in the world. The English word
ethos is derived directly from the Greek word *êthos,* which
means character. The dictionary definition of ethos makes
clear why I am suggesting that it is a good term for thinking
about the church in the world: "The disposition, character,
or fundamental values peculiar to a specific person, people,
culture, or movement."[2] Here is the "city built on a hill [that]
cannot be hid."

The challenge to the church is to understand its ethos.
What is its disposition and character, what are its fundamental values? Are they essentially those of the reign
of God, taught and practiced by Jesus, or do they come
from somewhere else? Has the church so internalized the
values and interests of culture or different classes of society that the line between the church and "the world" is
blurred to indistinctness? Difficult as it may be, radical

and continuing self-criticism seems a central task of the church that is "always reforming" and thus more likely to be always relevant.

Not surprisingly, our word *ethics* also comes from the Greek word for character, *ēthos*. The dictionary tells us that ethics refers to "a set of principles of right conduct. . . . a theory or a system of moral values."[3] Interestingly, the Chinese word for ethics, *lun li*, literally means the "logic or order of things." It raises the question as to what is the "order of things" in personal and communal life that leads to personal and communal well-being. Ethics, ethos, and *lun li* all point to the distinctive "character" of individuals or particular communities, stressing how individuals or communities should be and behave under certain social, cultural, and religious situations in order to realize the fundamental values of the community. Which is to say that the "principles of right conduct," the "system of moral values," that is to say, the ethics that lie at the core of a community's ethos, are not simply descriptive; they are prescriptive as well. Jesus' question in Luke 6:46 is apropos: "Why do you call me 'Lord, Lord,' and do not do what I tell you?"

Both the ethics and the ethos of a Christian community are inseparable from faith for the simple fact that our faith is faith in the particular God revealed by Jesus, a God who requires his followers to "do justice, love kindness, and walk humbly with your God" (Micah 6:8). These requirements are grounded in the nature of God as Jews and Christians have experienced God and should form the heart of any Christian community of faith.

Ethical behavior, that is, behavior that stems from the ethos of a Christian community of faith should not be confused with the "works righteousness" that was rejected by the Protestant Reformation. Ethical behavior earns no special merit from God and has no special saving reward. Ethical behavior simply has to do with being true to oneself as one comes to more deeply know oneself in God. According to Paul, God's Spirit is at work within us, transforming us into the image of Christ (2 Corinthians 3:18). As a result of this transformation, rather than being conformed to "the world," the community of faith is empowered to "discern what is the will of God" (Romans 12:2). Such a community follows Paul's advice: "If we live by the Spirit, let us also be guided by the Spirit" (Galatians 5:25). This has nothing to do with works righteousness. It has everything to do with living within the ethos of Jesus and following his ethics simply because it is right to who we are in God.

Let's consider a few questions before moving on to consider some texts that might help us unpack the ethos and ethics of Jesus.

1. What signs of the church's malaise and apathy have you experienced?

2. Why are you (or are you not) pessimistic about the state of the church in the contemporary world?

3. The demise of denominations has long been predicted. Do you see it happening or not, and why?

4. What are the theological implications of the apparent migration from essentially "confessional" religion to more "experiential" religion?

5. What forms might radical self-criticism in the church take?

6. What dangers might there be in radical self-criticism and how might they be avoided?

Discerning the Ethos and Ethics of Jesus

There are two kinds of texts in the Gospels that are helpful in attempting to discern the ethos and ethics of Jesus: discourses and parables that reflect Jesus' teaching of the rule of God and narrative texts about what Jesus did that serve to illustrate his teaching. For example, Jesus' parable of the great and all inclusive banquet in Luke 14 is illustrated in what John Dominic Crossan has called Jesus' practice of "open commensality,"[4] or sitting and eating at table with any and all. Here we find two characteristics of Jesus' ethos that should also be the ethos of communities of faith that claim to follow him: inclusiveness and hospitality. These characteristics remind us that for Jesus, "It is not enough to wait for a future kingdom; one must enter a present one here and now."[5]

Clues to the Ethos and Ethics of Jesus in the Lord's Prayer

There is no other prayer more familiar to Christians than the Lord's prayer. It is recited both in public worship and in private devotions. Because of its familiarity, however, its ethical implications tend to be lost. We recognize it as the prayer Jesus taught us to pray, but we often fail to recognize that through this prayer Jesus taught us about his ethos and thus about the ethos that is meant to shape the Christian life of faith.

According to Luke's version of the prayer, Jesus taught his followers to ask, "Your kingdom (rule) come" (Luke 11:2). Matthew interprets and clarifies Luke's meaning by reporting that Jesus followed this petition with: "Your will be done on earth as it is in heaven" (Matthew 6:10). Here is another intimation of the ethos of Jesus, commitment to the rule of God expressed in submission to the divine will. As Jesus declared,

"Not everyone who says to me, 'Lord, Lord,' will enter the kingdom of heaven, but only the one who does the will of my Father in heaven" (Matthew 7:21). This commitment to the rule of God is illustrated in the Garden of Gethsemane when Jesus, facing death because of his allegiance to the rule of God, "threw himself on the ground and prayed, "My Father, if it is possible, let this cup pass from me; yet not what I want but what you want" (Matthew 26:39). Or as Luke put it, "Not my will but yours be done" (Luke 22:41).

Communities of faith that share the ethos of Jesus self-consciously attempt to have "the same mind that was in Christ Jesus" who "emptied himself," "humbled himself," and "became obedient" to God's purposes (Philippians 2:5ff.). Jesus' way of being should be determinative of the church's way of being. Proclaiming the will of God on Sunday morning and saying "Amen" to it is one thing, doing it throughout the week is something else. Only communities of faith that struggle to be obedient as Jesus was will have any real credibility with their own members and the larger public.

There are other characteristics of Jesus' ethos to be found in this short prayer. When we pray for "daily bread" and to be saved from "the time of trial," we are expressing trust, a fundamental mark of those who submit themselves to the rule of God. Trust is faith or belief acted upon. When we pray to be forgiven as we forgive, we recognize the fundamental place of forgiveness in the community of faith and express our willingness to be both responsible and accountable in this regard. Words of forgiveness have no relevance apart from the experience of giving and receiving forgiveness. And if the words of Jesus on the cross in Luke's passion narrative bear on the ethos of Jesus, in the community of those who follow Jesus, the words of forgiveness are spoken before they are asked for: "Father forgive them; for they do not know what they are doing" (Luke 23:34).

Mark opens his gospel with a summary statement of Jesus' career when he writes: "Jesus came to Galilee, proclaiming the good news of God, and saying, 'The time is fulfilled, and the kingdom of God has come near; repent, and believe in the good news'" (Mark 1:14). Jesus considered his own practice a manifestation of the rule of God and considered the practice of those who followed him to also be a realization of the rule of God in the world (cf. Matthew 10:7–8).

Realizing the rule of God in the midst of the world is an ethical demand that the church has frequently failed to fulfill in the course of its history. One wonders if the difficulty of the task is not one of the reasons that many if not most Christians are content to leave the kingdom of God to some indeterminate future when God will do what is necessary to bring it about. That attitude, of course, creates a credibility gap between the church and those who hear its proclamation of the kingdom but do not see the proclamation translated into action in any credible way.

I do not think that Jesus was willing to wholly relegate the kingdom to some indeterminate future. While accepting to some degree the eschatological hopes of his time and tradition, he clearly believed that the rule of God could be found in his action and in the action of his followers. It is in the struggle (a not always successful struggle, but a struggle with integrity) that the community of faith becomes the city set on a hill that cannot be hid.

More Clues to the Ethos and Ethics of Jesus in the Beatitudes

The church over its two thousand years of existence has manifested more division than unity. The disunity in the church throughout its history seems to have been caused more by theological disputes and the struggle for both

ecclesiastical and temporal power than it has by honest dis-
agreements over how the church could best be an agent of
the rule of God. The proliferation of different and compet-
ing confessions, traditions, communions, and denominations, challenges theological arguments as to the unity of
the church, a unity given to the church by God in Jesus
Christ. The unity of the church is a heartening concept but
experience would suggest that, other than in abstract terms,
it will not be realized.

So, are we to resign ourselves to disunity, hostility, and
outright division in the "body of Christ"? Perhaps, but perhaps not. This is a soul-searching question. To the degree
that Christian churches are preoccupied with power and
prestige, disunity seems inevitable. To the degree, however,
that they practice love and compassion, movement toward
unity in the body of Christ through sharing in the ethos and
ethics of Jesus seems a real possibility.

Intimations of that ethos can be found in the so-called
"beatitudes" found in Matthew 5:3–12 and Luke 6:20–23.
These two sets of beatitudes are similar and yet different.
Luke's list of blessings (which most scholars see as more
original in form than Matthew's) is shorter than Matthew's
and seems to address social inequities. Matthew's longer
list seems to add an overtly religious dimension to Luke's
social concern. It has been suggested that Matthew has
spiritualized Luke's shorter list, thus diminishing the force
of Luke's social consciousness. That, however, is not the
case. The social realities with which Luke is concerned are
indeed spiritual realities in the ethos of Jesus, and Matthew
has made their spiritual dimension more explicit.

The English word *beatitude* is derived from the Latin
beâtus which means happy or blessed, a literal rendering
of the Greek *makários*. As we read through the beatitudes,
we might well understand them to be saying, "Happy are
those, blessed are those, fortunate are those who participate

in the ethos of Jesus and live by his ethics." We will take a brief look at the parallel beatitudes in Luke and Matthew and then briefly suggest additional marks of the ethos of Jesus found in Matthew's longer list.

Happy Are the Poor

The ethos of Jesus is that of the rule or kingdom of God and in the first beatitude we are told: "Blessed are you who are poor, for yours is the kingdom of God;" (Luke 6:20) "Blessed are the poor in spirit, for theirs is the kingdom of heaven." (Matthew 5:3). Matthew and Luke essentially mean the same thing. "Centuries before Jesus, poor in the vocabulary of Israel had come to mean something deeper than lacking in wealth. As *rich* easily became a synonym for "self-sufficient" and then "arrogant," so *poor* came to signify "humble" and "trusting." It was proverbial to speak of those poor in the goods of this world as rich in faith and heirs of the kingdom of heaven."[6] The understanding of the poor as the "righteous" and the rich as "wicked" (cf. Psalm 37) is perhaps an idealization of the poor, but it is grounded in political and economic realities.

The beatitudes affirm that "the poor" and the "poor in spirit," those who have little in the way of material wealth and those who, in their humility and trust, acknowledge God as their only resource are included in the kingdom, not excluded. Those at the margins of the social, political, and economic world are in the center of the circle of God's love. This does not mean that the rich are excluded, unless, of course, in their self-sufficiency and arrogance, they exclude themselves. Or, as all three of the synoptic gospels claim, Jesus said, "Again I tell you, it is easier for a camel to go through the eye of a needle than for someone who is rich to enter the kingdom of God" (Matthew 19:24).

As some Latin American liberation theologians have stressed, in the rule of God there seems to be a "preferential option for the poor." The church that shares the ethos of Jesus practices an ethics of inclusion. The normally excluded poor are valued as beloved of God and included. In the community of faith, poverty matters and intentional action on behalf of the poor is a sign of the kingdom. In such communal action, the "rich" have an opportunity to experience and learn that poverty of spirit in which the rule of God is theirs as well. The kind of questions the church might ask to increase both its relevance and credibility among people who have been turned off by power struggles, doctrinal disputes, and the clash of creeds are such as these: What are we doing with the poor? What are we doing about poverty? What does Jesus teach in the Gospels that drive us to take poverty seriously?

Happy Are Those Who Mourn and Weep

Both "mourning" (Matthew 5:4) and "weeping" (Luke 6:21b) refer to "grief caused by both personal sin and loss and social evil and oppression."[7] To participate in the ethos of Jesus, the community of faith must share his grief over both personal sin/evil and social sin/evil.

It may be an oversimplification, but many churches and Christians seem to think, preach, and act as if personal sin and social evil were two separate things. They do not seem to realize that personal sin does not remain personal, but is externalized in the many forms of social evil. Conversely, the root of social evil is personal sin.

Again, although it may be an oversimplification, churches can be divided into two broad categories—those who "weep" over social and systemic evil, and those who weep over personal sin and its consequences. Neither type fully shares in the ethos of Jesus nor practices the ethics of

Jesus. Many mainline churches are ready to take an active role in demonstrating against social evil and work passionately against exploitation and oppression be it political, economic, racial, sexual, class, or religious. In their passion against these evils, however, they share a tendency to forget the reality of personal sin and thus are blinded to their own culpability in the systemic evils they fight against.

There are, on the other hand, Christians and churches who are so preoccupied with personal sin that their religious focus is narrowed to the desire to be saved from what they believe to be God's judgment and punishment. As a result, they are less aware of the dynamics of social and systemic evil, attributing such to the personal sin of others. The result is passionate involvement in one's own spiritual well-being and a bad case of myopia with respect to one's responsibility for social well-being.

For a community of faith to participate in the ethics of Jesus, its spiritual focus must broaden to the point that it clearly sees the interrelatedness of personal sin and systemic evil and "weeps" over both. Such weeping is an impetus to repentance and remedial action, and in that, the beatitude promises, there is both comfort and joy, and we might add, credibility and relevance.

Happy Are Those Who Hunger and Thirst

In Luke's Gospel, Jesus proclaims: "Blessed are you who are hungry now . . ." (Luke 6:21). One assumes he is speaking about those who are literally hungry, and one presumes that he is also talking about those who are figuratively hungry. Matthew develops this presumption by declaring, "Blessed are those who hunger and thirst for righteousness sake . . ." (Matthew 5:6).

Just as poverty matters in the rule of God, so do hunger and thirst. Like poverty, they are to be eliminated through the action of God's people who "hunger and thirst for righteousness." It is, of course, the righteousness of God and not our own righteousness that we are to hunger and thirst for. The fact that many churches seek their own righteousness rather than the righteousness of God is a significant factor in the church's loss of credibility and relevance. The Greek word *dikaiosune*, translated as "righteousness" in the New Revised Standard Version (NRSV) is perhaps better translated as "fair and equitable dealing," or simply "justice." What then is God's justice in the context of these two beatitudes?

When the people of a church who are short of material means hunger and thirst for justice, they are seeking to have "their basic needs for food met, but it goes on to include a desire to see God's standards [of fairness and equitableness] established and obeyed in every area of life."[8] What is "right" or "just" with God is that those without "food," and all that the word symbolizes, have access to "food" and that includes both those in the church and those outside the church. If the church that lacks "food" only hungers and thirsts for itself, it is not sharing the ethics of Jesus and is thus not a sign of God's rule to the world. Jesus understood that God's graciousness and compassion extend to all (cf. Matthew 5:43ff.). But when the church claims the right to "food" for those outside as well as inside the church, and struggles to realize that right, it is again that city set on a hill that cannot be hid.

What then about churches that enjoy prosperity? What would participating in the ethos of God, where people of faith hunger and thirst for justice, look like for them? I suggest it would look like sharing, advocacy, and activism in the search for fairness and equitableness. One would expect such a church to hold as a core value Paul's expectation of the relatively well-off church in Corinth vis-à-vis the impoverished church in Jerusalem:

I do not mean that there should be relief for others and pressure on you, but it is a question of a fair balance between your present abundance and their need, so that their abundance may be for your need, in order that there may be a fair balance. As it is written, "The one who had much did not have too much, and the one who had little did not have too little." (2 Corinthians 8:13–15)

Happy Are Those Who Suffer

"Blessed are you when people hate you, and when they exclude you, revile you, and defame you on account of the Son of Man" (Luke 6:23). Matthew concurs (5:11). Following Jesus under the rule of God could well, indeed, probably will lead to suffering. There is a danger here; suffering can all too easily be seen as a goal of faithfulness rather than a consequence of faithfulness. I am not at suggesting (as some "martyrs" have suggested) that suffering is to be sought. I am simply suggesting that it ought not to be avoided.

As we have seen, the human tendency toward sin (which Luther described as the state of being curved in on yourself) means that the rule of God proclaimed and practiced by Jesus is radically counterintuitive and thus radically countercultural. It is to be expected, then, that churches and individuals who live by the ethics of Jesus will be "reviled" and "persecuted" as Jesus was by those who are guardians of the conventional.

A willingness—not a desire for, but a willingness—to suffer in order not to betray the rule of God is the beating heart of Jesus' ethics. Suffering here is understood not as a mark of personal or communal righteousness but as a mark of solidarity, of being with, of accompanying all those who suffer unjustly. Such churches and people of faith are indeed blessed for "theirs is the kingdom of heaven," (Matthew 5:10) and their credibility and relevance are immense.

More Clues to the Ethos and Ethics of Jesus

Matthew's longer list of beatitudes includes blessings for the meek, the merciful, the pure of heart, and the peacemakers. They will, respectively, inherit the earth, receive mercy, see God, and be called children of God. Of such is the kingdom of God. Of such should be the church of God.

To be meek is often confused with being submissive, but in the ethos of Jesus, to be meek is to be patient, humble, and gentle. To be merciful is often confused with overlooking the faults of others, but in the ethos of Jesus it is to be compassionate regardless of the fault of others. To be pure of heart is often confused with personal holiness, but in the ethos of Jesus, it is single-mindedness in pursuit of God's righteousness. To be a peacemaker is often confused with the solving of conflict, but in the ethos of Jesus, to be a peacemaker is to struggle to remove the causes of conflict.

For churches in our time to have credibility with both their membership and with those who look on from the outside and to be relevant to the real lives real people lead, it is sharing the ethos and practicing the ethics of Jesus and not doctrinal disputes and ecclesiastical arguments that will pave the way.

And now for a few questions before moving on to consider the mission of the church.

1. Does the idea of the "ethos and ethics of Jesus" as the core value for a community of faith make sense or not? Why?

2. What might be the theological and practical implications of affirming Jesus' way of being as determinative of the church's way of being?

3. What forms might "open commensality" or "open church" take in a congregation?

4. Programmatically, what would an "ethics of inclusion" involve in a congregation?

5. Read through the gospels and look for illustrations in the narrative texts that illustrate Jesus' teaching in the Lord's Prayer and the Beatitudes.

7. What Is Christian Mission?

From its inception, Christianity has understood itself as a "missionary religion" and has justified its missionary expansion by reference to its founder. The book of Acts, written some fifty to sixty years after Jesus' death, recalls Jesus telling his disciples, "You will be my witnesses in Jerusalem, in all Judea, and Samaria, and to the ends of the world" (Acts 1:8). The Gospel of Matthew, also written some fifty to sixty years after Jesus' crucifixion, closes with the risen Christ telling his followers, "Go therefore and make disciples of all nations, baptizing them in the name of the Father and of the Son and of the Holy Spirit, and teaching them to obey everything that I have commanded you" (Matthew 28:19–20a).

Although these texts can be understood in very different ways, the overriding interpretation has tended toward Christian triumphalism and aggressive proselytism. In considering the scope of Christian mission in the twenty-first century, perhaps we should wonder if these and other texts might support a more humble and credible approach to our culturally and religiously pluralistic world. For example, in the text of Acts above, could not being a witness of Jesus be taken as living a public life that affirms and demonstrates the rule of God that shaped who and how Jesus was?

In the message of Matthew quoted above, could not "making disciples of all nations" and "teaching them to obey everything I have commanded you" be interpreted as the call to create inclusive and intentional communities of faith who demonstrate in their life together Jesus' commandment that we love God above all things and our neighbors as ourselves? Would this not be a more credible and effective approach to the world than interpreting the text in a triumphalist way? Would not such a community of faith be that city set on a hill that can not be hid? Would not such a church eschew the aggressive and coercive proselytism that has characterized mission, and thus draw people into the community through the unique quality of its life together under the rule of God?

If the Christian church has a mission, is it to convert the world through one means or another to its system of belief and ecclesiastical institutions, or is it to serve the world as an agent of God's rule? Is it to draw the world into itself or is it to immerse itself into the world as a change agent? Jesus' comparison of the kingdom of God with yeast suggests the latter (Matthew 13:33, Luke 13:21).

The "Rome Complex"

When the book of Acts records Jesus as sending his disciples to "the ends of the world," it is safe to presume that its author, Luke, had in mind the extent of the Roman Empire in general and Rome in particular. It was a bold statement and a reflection of what was actually happening as Luke wrote. The Christian faith—or as Luke would put it, the Way—had moved beyond the borders of the Holy Land with its eyes on Rome.

Rome's tentacles reached everywhere in the ancient Mediterranean world. Roman hegemony in the Middle East was unchallenged. Rome meant irresistible power. Rome meant conquest and subjugation. Rome meant wealth. Rome meant prestige and privilege. Rome meant patronage. Rome meant control of commerce. One could go on, but this is enough to suggest that "Rome" became a metaphor—positive or negative depending on who said it—of the destiny of humankind.

The early church lived in a Roman world, and its life together was lived over against that world. Indeed, to a great degree, the Christian way of life was a critique of the presumptions of Roman power, which in part explains the persecutions of the church by Rome. Things changed forever, however, with the Edict of Milan in 313 C.E., which mandated toleration of Christians in the Roman Empire and eventually led to Christianity's assumption of the role of state religion.

It could be argued that when the victorious soldiers of Emperor Constantine rode into battle with the *Chi Rho*, the monogram of Christ, emblazoned on their shields and banners, the fate of the church was unfortunately sealed. The pretensions of Rome became in time the pretensions of the church. The church not only sought the trappings of temporal power, but just as Rome never questioned its hegemonic rights vis-à-vis other states, the church has for the most part not questioned its hegemonic rights vis-à-vis other religions.

If I may coin an expression, we might say that over the centuries and into the present, large parts of the church have suffered from a "Rome complex." In psychiatry, a complex is "a group of related, often repressed ideas and impulses that compel characteristic or habitual patterns of thought, feelings, and behavior."[1] That being the case, it is both easy to understand what the Rome complex is and how it has functioned in often unconscious ways to hinder, if not prevent, an internal Christian critique of the church's hegemonic pretensions, both temporal and spiritual, pretensions that have given "mission" a bad name both inside and outside the church.

It is one thing to reject the Rome complex abstractly and intellectually. More mission conferences, seminars, and study groups have done this in the past century than could easily be counted. The annals of mission literature over the past one hundred years are replete with admissions of *mea culpa* responsibility for the worst excesses of the missionary expansion of the church. And yet, the "habitual patterns of thought, feelings, and behavior" that led to those excesses are not easily exorcised. The Rome complex is too deeply ingrained in the collective psyche of the church.

Mission Impossible?

Does this make mission impossible? Perhaps, but perhaps not. On the one hand, mission in the ways suggested by the Rome complex is no longer possible. The world outside the church thoroughly rejects it, and inside the church growing numbers reject it as well. Many of those who have suffered with the Rome complex are like addicts who have finally come to recognize and own their addiction—they know they are sick—and yet they can't seem to find the strength or inner resources to overcome the addiction.

On the other hand, models of mission—grounded not in hegemonic dreams but in the realities of interdependent cooperation with other cultural and religious institutions for the sake of expanding the ethos and ethics of God's rule that Jesus proclaimed and practiced—seem not only possible, but are also potentially powerful expressions in the larger community of divine justice, compassion, and love. Which is to say that Christian communities of faith have a pretty serious reconstructive task to tend to before they attempt mission-related tasks. They need to reconstruct themselves as communities of the Way. The church needs to tend to what Jesus was about and begin leaving the trappings of Rome behind.

As those suffering from addictive behavior, who come to realize their lack of self-sufficiency and so become involved in a twelve-step program, find resources for health and freedom in a "higher power," the church suffering from the Rome complex would do well to repudiate its pretensions to self-sufficiency and truly open itself to the power of God's holy and transforming Spirit.

Now for a few questions for reflection before looking for missional insights in narratives about Jesus.

1. Which do you think is a more correct understanding of mission: mission as inducements to conversion or mission as representing the ethos and ethics of Jesus in the world? Why?

2. In what ways might Christianity's self-consciousness as a "missionary religion," impede "mission" as representing the ethos and ethics of Jesus in the world?

3. What, if any, room is there in Christian mission for proselytism?

4. In what way is the notion of a "Rome complex" in the churches helpful (or not) in approaching the self-critical tasks needed if the church is to be "always reforming?"

5. What is at stake for any church that surrenders claims to hegemony in a culturally and religiously pluralistic context?

6. What might be at stake both theologically and practically in shifting the church's understanding of mission from one

that primarily sees mission as drawing the world into the church's belief systems and structures to one that primarily sees mission as the church's immersion in the world as an agent of change?

Mission as Spreading Freedom

Paul declared in ringing tones, "For freedom Christ has set us free" (Galatians 5:1). Jesus himself declared, "If you continue in my word, you are truly my disciples; and you will know the truth, and the truth will make you free." As I mentioned in chapter 5, when Jesus inaugurated his ministry in his hometown of Nazareth, he chose a text from the prophet Isaiah to indicate what he was about: "The Spirit of the Lord is upon me, because he has anointed me to bring good news to the poor. He has sent me to proclaim release to the captives and recovery of sight to the blind, to let the oppressed go free, to proclaim the year of the Lord's favor" (Luke 4:18–19). Again the theme is freedom. Freedom from poverty and exclusion; freedom from captivity, freedom from blindness; freedom from oppression; freedom from economic disenfranchisement.[2] Jesus' program was about freedom, all of which suggests that if Christian mission is to be both credible and relevant, it too must be about freedom.

Maybe What Jesus Really Said Was, "What do you think that I am doing?"

It could be argued that early Christological developments are reflected in Jesus' question to the disciples, "Who do you say that I am?" and Peter's response on their (the church's?) behalf, "You are the Messiah, the Son of the living God" (Matthew 16:15–16). One could call this confession of the church, written in the eighties or nineties of the first century, Christology in its embryonic form.

This Christological embryo, to extend the metaphor, was nurtured in the womb of the early church, brought to term in 325 C.E. in the Nicene Creed, and grew to adulthood in Europe in the centuries that followed. It represents the Christology that most Christians embrace today and is the cornerstone, to change metaphors, of the Christian mission to convert non-Christians to the one true faith. Conversion occurs when non-Christians answer Jesus' question, "Who do you say I am?" with Peter's (the church's) answer, "You are the Messiah, the (only) Son of the living God." Christian exclusivity is encapsulated in this confession.

But would Jesus of Nazareth have asked that question expecting that answer? I suspect not. You will recall from our discussion in chapter 3, that the imprisoned John the Baptist sent some of his followers to ask Jesus, "Are you the one who is to come or should we look for another?" That is, "Are you the Messiah?" Jesus did not say either yes or no. Indeed, he seemed uninterested in the question. He responded by pointing to what he was doing: "Go and tell John, what you hear and see: the blind receive their sight, the lame walk, the lepers are cleansed, the deaf hear, the dead are raised, and the poor have good news brought to them. And blessed is anyone who takes no offense at me" (Matthew 11:2–6).

Based on this story and Jesus' inaugural speech from Luke 4, I would suggest an imaginative reconstruction of the narrative in Matthew 16 and its parallels in Mark and Luke. The setting of the story can be the same, the lonely road to the village of Caesarea Philippi. The cast of the story stays the same: Jesus still asks the question, and Peter still answers for the disciples. Everything is the same—except the question. Not "Who do you say that I am?" but "What do you think that I am doing?"

In my not so-fanciful reconstruction, the question shifts from a concern with who Jesus is to a concern with what he does, from his person to his ministry, from his "credentials" as the Messiah, the Son of the living God, to the rule of God he strove for. What we may take as the "pre-Christological Jesus" does not seem worried about who people take him to be. What he is really worried about is how they consistently seem to misunderstand what he is doing.

The Son of Man Came Not to Be Served but to Serve

The authors of the Gospels in story after story, in incident after incident, dwell on the fact that Jesus' followers often failed to understand what he was doing. Could it be because what he said and what he did represented such a radical break with what they believed to be true about the kingdom that they simply couldn't get their minds around it? If freedom is at the heart of Jesus' program, then growing freedom from conventional values, thought, and behavior seems to be a prerequisite to experiencing his liberating power.

To give just one example, at one point well into his ministry, Jesus found the disciples arguing over who would sit at his right and at his left when he came into his kingdom. They were looking for the place of power, prestige, glory. They seemed to have a bad case of the Rome complex. Jesus is reported to have said to his disciples: "You know that the rulers of the Gentiles lord it over them, and their great ones are tyrants over them. It will not be so among you; but whoever wishes to be great among you must be your servant, and whoever wishes to be first among you must be your slave; just as the Son of Man came not to be served but to serve . . ." (Matthew 20:25–28).

This text may reflect leadership struggles in the early church, but that is not the point. The point is that, be it from the struggles of the early church or from the mouth of Jesus, the story reflects a radical change in the under-standing of what leadership means that is typical of Jesus' ethics. Leadership in the rule of God is not in the future, and it has nothing to do with power, glory, and privilege. Second, leadership in the rule of God is now, and it has to do with serving the needs of others.

There was little in conventional ways of thinking to prepare the disciples for this kind of leadership, and their failure to understand is quite understandable. Jesus, meta-phorically speaking, was driving the chariot south, but the disciples were going north, to use a Chinese idiom. A church interested in doing mission in the way of Jesus will struggle to free itself from conventional values, thought, and behavior before it moves out into our pluralistic world in an attempt to bring freedom to others. To the degree that it is successful, it will be a model of genuine servant leadership.

Freedom from Captivity to Greed

The reality of economic injustice is not news. When Jesus declared, "You always have the poor with you" (John 12:8), he was neither justifying nor rationalizing poverty, he was simply observing reality. Although it may seem simplistic, Jesus apparently saw economic injustice as a result of the captivity of the human spirit to greed. The antidote to eco-nomic injustice then is to be found in human freedom from greed. That certainly does not sound sophisticated enough to tackle the immense problems of economic oppression and exploitation occasioned by economic globalization. And yet, given what we said in the last chapter about the relationship between personal sin and systemic evil, it may be a good place for a church that wants to be in mission to begin. To draw from the language in Jesus' inaugural speech in Luke 4, Jesus' mission included setting free those who were captive to greed for the sake of their own spirituality, but also with the intention that those who suffered from economic oppression would thereby be set free.

A positive example is in the case of the fraudulent tax collector, Zacchaeus. Through his encounter with Jesus, his attitudes toward wealth and the poor were radically changed: "Look, half of my possessions, Lord, I will give to the poor; and if I have defrauded anyone of anything, I will pay back four times as much" (Luke 19:8). By giving half of his possessions to the poor, he demonstrated his conversion to Jesus' ethics. By giving back four times as much to those he had defrauded, Zacchaeus went way beyond what the law required, which was only restitution plus 20 percent (Numbers 5:5–7). This is another indication that he had been freed from greed, from the undue desire to acquire and possess more than he either needed or deserved. Jesus response to Zacchaeus is instructive, "Today salvation has come to this house . . ." (19:9). There is no hint here that Jesus is referring to salvation as eternal life. Rather, he is pointing to the healing of Zacchaeus's spirit—salvation in the here and now through a radical change in his relationship to both wealth and the poor.

A failed, but instructive, example of Jesus' attempt to free the human spirit from captivity to greed is found in the well-known but not very well-liked story of Jesus and the rich young man who came to Jesus wanting to know what he must do to "have eternal life." Jesus said to him, "If you wish to be perfect, go, sell your possessions, and give the money to the poor, and you will have treasure in heaven; then come, follow me." When the young man heard this word, "he went away grieving, for he had many possessions." No radical change there, no conversion toward the poor. Jesus' words to the rich young man sound strikingly similar to the teaching of the Buddha that, "The avaricious do not go to heaven, the foolish do not extol charity. The wise one, however, rejoicing in charity, becomes thereby happy in the beyond."[3]

Jesus certainly viewed a person's relationship to both wealth and the poor as a spiritual matter of great consequence, both for the individual and the community. In his counsel to his followers that they not worry about food or clothing (metaphors for material possessions), his argument rests on trust in the God who creates and sustains life. With respect to wealth and possessions, and the supposed security they provide, he tells them that, "It is the nations of the world that strive after all these things, and your Father knows that you need them. Instead, strive for his kingdom, and these things will be given to you as well" (Luke 12:30–31).

If it is the "nations of the world" that strive for wealth and material possessions, then it must be admitted that in large part the church is one of the nations of the world. Again, the church must get its own house in order before trying to get the house of the world in order. Credible and relevant Christian mission in a world where greed and acquisitiveness have been enshrined as culturally normative values is impossible as long as the life of the church and its membership reflect those values. The church's ability to be a credible dynamic force for economic justice will be proportionate to the degree to which its internal reality demonstrates its acceptance of Jesus' radical view of wealth.

Of course, important as it is, economic justice is not the only thing at stake in Jesus' program to free people from their captivity to greed. Jesus advice to a man overly concerned with wealth and property is to the point: "Take care! Be on your guard against all kinds of greed; for one's life does not consist in the abundance of possessions" (Luke 12:15). It seems to be the case in most religious traditions that spiritual seekers have an intuitive sense that their quest for God and an authentically human life requires the development of a simple life with respect to wealth and possessions. Or as Jesus put it with startling clarity, "You cannot serve God and wealth" (Luke 6:13b). The church has nothing to say to anyone in this regard as long as its institutional life serves not God but wealth. And if the church cannot speak to issues of authentic human life, what does it have to say?

Freedom from Captivity to Religion

It may seem radical to suggest that both people of faith and people of no faith need to be freed from captivity to religion, but upon further thought it seems as if religion has done as much if not more to enslave the human spirit than to set it free. Volumes could be written on the violence done to human bodies, human minds, and human spirits by religious institutions in the name of "truth" or "God." All too often religion is used to control and restrict human thought and behavior rather than to empower human freedom in seeking, experiencing, and expressing God.

Interestingly enough, our English word *religion* is derived from the Latin verb *religâre* which means to "tie fast, to bind, or to bind together." Religion serves to bind people to a belief system, to rites and rituals, and to a religious community and its hierarchy. History is replete with instances of religions using physical, psychological, and spiritual coercion to "bind" people and to keep them bound. Religion, in short, makes people unfree. It could be, and has been, argued that in complete submission to one's religion, one gains true freedom. That, however, seems a bit self-serving.

The Gospel narratives give us a Jesus who seemed remarkably free from his own religion and who took it upon himself to free people from its legalistic control, which he saw as diminishing the meaning of life. The Gospels give many accounts of his setting aside much of the binding codes of Hebrew tradition, which controlled both behavior and relationships such as Sabbath laws, food laws, and cleanliness or purity laws. He showed an openness to Gentiles, Samaritans, women, and children, and he encouraged people to seek the kingdom or rule of God not in the temple, but in daily life and relationships.

The way of God, he suggested, could be found by considering the birds of the air and the flowers of the field as well, if not better than in observing the teaching of the Pharisees who he described as "blind guides," and "blind fools." He called them hypocrites who "tithe mint, dill, and cumin, and have neglected the weightier matters of the law: justice and mercy and faith." It is these latter, he argues, that they "ought to have practiced" (Matthew 23:23). Indeed, the whole of Matthew 23 is an extended critique of legalistic religion and its negative binding power.

It is difficult, if not impossible, to imagine a religion without religion, and yet one is tempted to think that in Jesus' attempt to relate people directly to God as a benevolent, compassionate, trustworthy "father," he was imagining just that—faith not bound by religion. The movement away from "religion" without abandoning "spirituality" is seen in the increasing numbers of people who confess to being "spiritual" but vigorously deny being "religious." If Jesus did imagine and practice a faith not bound by religion, we can perhaps hear echoes of it in Dietrich Bonhoeffer's notion (in *Letters and Papers from Prison*) of a "religionless Christianity."

I am not at all sure how we might go about this, but I am willing to say that it has something to do with what I have been advocating for, namely the theological and practical repudiation by the church of the "Rome complex" and the intentional attempt by the community of faith to share the ethos and ethics of Jesus. Both are preconditions for Christian credibility and relevance in our post-modern world.

1. Do you agree that credible Christian mission is impossible without a theological and practical repudiation by the church of the Rome complex? Why or why not?

2. Is "freedom" adequate for describing the goal of Christian engagement with the world? Why is it or why isn't it?

3. What steps might a church take to begin internalizing Jesus' values with respect to wealth and possessions?

4. Is "religionless faith" a contradiction in terms? Why or why not?

5. What theological and practical dangers might there be in "religionless faith"? How might they be protected against?

6. Would "religionless faith" mean the demise of denominations? If so, what might take their place?

8. What Is Spirituality?

Although the word *spirituality* has a venerable Catholic history, it is only beginning in the 1960s that the word *spirituality* began to be heard more regularly in Protestant churches, perhaps due to the influence in Protestant circles of the Catholic spiritual writer, Thomas Merton. Gradually, spirituality began to be used interchangeably with the venerable Protestant term, "the life of faith." The term has now has been mainstreamed in Protestantism, although the word today seems to have a considerably wider range of meaning than "the life of faith."

With the Hippie movement, the human potential movement, the Jesus People movement, the charismatic or neo-Pentecostal movement, and the New Age movement, the term spirituality spilled out of the churches and entered the free-flowing mainstream of American culture. Spirituality now seems to mean as many things as there are people who use the word. It has become an intensely individualistic pursuit that speaks to the longing of the human spirit for experience of and connection to the divine.

We might want to raise the question, however, as to whether spirituality can be a purely individualistic matter or whether it demands a communal or shared dimension as well. Spirituality is a profound experience of connection, not isolation, and as we shall see, the life of the spirit connects us to more than God.

Anything and everything, it seems, can be "spiritual." From planting rice in a paddy field to eating it in a bowl; from baking bread to eating it with a piece of cheese, and perhaps a glass of wine, with good friends; from making pottery to working in a cubicle; from sexual intercourse to gardening; from sitting in meditation to jogging; from listening to music to making music to singing to writing poetry to painting; from washing dishes to chopping carrots; from studying the macrocosm to studying the microcosm; and according to the 1970s best seller, *Zen and the Art of Motorcycle Maintenance*, from riding to maintaining a motorcycle: anything, it seems, can be spiritual if it is done with the right awareness, the right attitude, the right "spirit." Which, of course, raises the question: what is the right awareness, the right attitude, the right spirit?

The fact that practically everything can be experienced spiritually is an indication that to be human is to be a spiritual creature. Throughout this book, I have been suggesting a fundamental spiritual reality, an innate, if often undeveloped or underdeveloped, human awareness or intuition of the sacred in itself and within creation. We are spiritual people by nature. Which is precisely why the bookstores are filled with books, CDs, and DVDs all designed to teach techniques to get in touch with our spiritual nature and gain "control" over it in order to secure for ourselves the abundant life, no matter how we define it.

Wherever you find something integral to human nature, you will find it being turned into a commodity, which usually serves to debase it. Such has certainly been the case with spirituality in this post-modern era. The result, of course, is that although there are some gems on the bookshelves, most of what you will find there under spirituality appeals not to our spiritual nature, but to our self-absorption and selfishness—things that genuine spirituality seeks to eliminate! How to be happy, how to be prosperous, how to be assertive, how to be healed, how to be successful; essentially how to manipulate the sacred for your own sake, is the theme of all too many books ostensibly about spirituality.

In spite of what we might call the commercialization of spirituality, there are countless people seeking to live a truly more spiritual life, trying to connect more deeply with the sacred "out there" and "within themselves" in order both to fulfill their humanity and to be a positive spiritual influence in their community.

> From many quarters of the world, voices are calling for increased attention to spirituality. These voices are diverse. The term spirituality has been used to describe everything from an appreciation of eastern religions and the practice of yoga to keeping journals, eating a vegetarian diet, sojourning in a wilderness, engaging in political resistance, practicing nonviolence, and praying quietly in silence. Yet within the variety of meanings, there is a fundamental concern for the care and nurture of the human spirit that we can recognize, not simply in the cries of the unchurched or the esoteric, but in members of our own churches as well.[1]

It is for such folks that this chapter is written.

God's Spirit over the Surface of the Water

It is not uncommon for Christian thinking about spirituality to begin with the biblical story of humankind being created in God's image (Genesis 1:26). One wonders, however, if this is the best place to start. Beginning with the story of men and women being created in the image of God has tended to send Christian thinking in two directions, one positive and one not so positive.

On the positive side, recall what was said in chapter 5 about the biblical understanding of a level of correspondence between God, the creator, and humankind, God's creatures, which allows for both divine disclosure and human receptivity to that which is disclosed. This correspondence between God and humans is traced to humankind's creation "in the image of God." It is a fundamental assumption of Christian spirituality.

On the negative side, however, the notion of being created in the image of God has led to humans understanding themselves as being at the apex of the hierarchy of God's creation. Following the account of humankind's creation in the image of God, the story goes on to say: "Be fruitful and multiply, and fill the earth and subdue it; and have dominion over the fish of the sea and over the birds of the air and over every living thing that moves upon the earth" (Genesis 1:28). Within much of Christian thought, there has been a hubristic tendency to view such texts as license to use creation as a means to human ends rather than seeing creation as an end in itself. Humans as spiritual creatures who alone were created in the image of God stand over against the rest of creation and exercise "dominion." The consequences of such spiritual pride and arrogance are obvious—the degradation and destruction of the non-human world for the supposed benefit of the human world.

There is another theological price to pay for placing humankind at the apex of the hierarchy of creation, that is to say, the Christian religion has come to be understood mainly within the themes of the fall of humankind and the redemption of humankind. Unlike some religious traditions, Christianity has a very human-centered theology and this has had disastrous consequences for both the non-human world as well as for Christianity's and the West's approach to indigenous cultures. One suspects that rather than keeping an essentially human-centered theology, Christianity needs to move toward a creation-centered theology. All of this suggests that the creation of humankind in the image of God may not be the best place to begin thinking about spirituality.

We should trace our steps further back to the very beginning of the creation story where it is said: "In the beginning when God created the heavens and the earth, the earth was a formless void and darkness covered the face of the deep, while a wind [or breath or spirit] from God swept over the face of the waters" (Genesis 1:1–2). The critical phrase in this verse is *ruah elohim*. The expression can be variously translated as "wind of God," "breath of God," or "Spirit of God" and connotes the creative, enlivening, inspiriting power of God.[2]

The creative, enlivening, inspiriting presence and power of God "in the beginning" is where we should begin a theology of spirituality. The whole creation—not just humankind—is brought into being by God. The creation of humankind is but one event in a series of events that constitute creation. Of course, creation would not be complete if human beings were left out, but the same can be said of every other creature. Would creation be complete without the sun, the moon, and the stars? Is it finished if it is not filled with trees and plants, flowers and vegetables, nuts and berries? Could creation be accomplished without mountains and meadows in which all kinds of animals roam and play? Is creation still creation if there are no rivers and oceans in which fishes and other sea creatures live?

Here it is worth quoting Psalm 104 at length.

You [God] make springs gush forth in the valleys;
they flow between the hills,
giving drink to every wild animal;
the wild asses quench their thirst.
By the streams the birds of the air have their habitation;
they sing among the branches.
From your lofty abode you water the mountains;
the earth is satisfied with the fruit of your work.
You cause the grass to grow for the cattle,

and plants for people to use,
to bring forth food from the earth,
and wine to gladden the human heart,
oil to make the face shine,
and bread to strengthen the human heart.
The trees of the LORD are watered abundantly,
the cedars of Lebanon that he planted.
In them the birds build their nests;
the stork has its home in the fir trees.
The high mountains are for the wild goats;
the rocks are a refuge for the coneys [rabbits].
You have made the moon to mark the seasons;
the sun knows its time for setting.
You make darkness, and it is night,
when all the animals of the forest come creeping out.
The young lions roar for their prey,
seeking their food from God.
When the sun rises, they withdraw
and lie down in their dens.
People go out to their work
and to their labor until the evening.
O LORD, how manifold are your works!
In wisdom you have made them all;
the earth is full of your creatures. (Psalm 104:10–24)

Notice the place given to humankind in this text, and you may be surprised to notice that there is remarkable parity between humans and non-humans in the care God gives to creation. "In wisdom [God] has made them all." In God's economy there is a beautiful symmetry between humans and non-humans. All alike are *inspirited*. To return to Psalm 104:

These all look to you
to give them their food in due season;
when you give to them, they gather it up;

when you open your hand, they are filled with good
    things.
When you hide your face, they are dismayed;
when you take away their breath, they die
and return to their dust.
When you send forth your spirit, [or breath] they are
*   created;*
and you renew the face of the ground.
(27–30, emphasis added)

Although creation stories in the Hebrew Bible do not specifically say that God created all things in God's own image, I do not think it is theologically far-fetched to imagine that in creating all things God imparts something of God's own self to them. If we do not press the analogy too far, God can be likened to an artisan making a bamboo vase or a rice bowl. An artisan's craft is far removed from the mass production of manufacturing machines. A bamboo vase or a rice bowl becomes an artistic masterpiece when the artisan "creates" it in his or her own image, as it were, that is, imparting what he or she is to the bamboo vase or the rice bowl in the making of it. The result is not just a bamboo vase or a rice bowl. It bears the marks of what the artisan is and stands for. In this sense, the bamboo vase or the rice bowl is created in the image of the artisan and bears the spirit of the artisan.

It might be argued that a creation-centered theology, which sees all things as inspirited, is demeaning to human beings. Does it not put humans on an equal footing with the non-human world vis-à-vis God? I think it probably does, at least with respect to grace, care, blessing, divine love. And why would that be a bad thing? If we could internalize such a truth, we might begin to experience a profound, and shall we say redemptive, respect for all creation. No matter how much we may revere God, there is no truly Christian spirituality apart from such respect for *all* creation. I suspect that such respect is what God desired "in the beginning" when the Spirit hovered over the waters.

Our reflection has suggested that, in a profound sense, there is no ultimate ontological distinction between humans and non-humans. There is in the biblical understanding, however, a functional distinction. Humans have dominion. Dominion is the language of royalty, of sovereignty. God was conceived of as Israel's king and ultimate dominion over creation belongs to God alone. However, in the Hebrew understanding, God delegated dominion over creation to humankind. Psalm 8 is to the point:

> When I look at your heavens,
> the work of your fingers,
> the moon and the stars that
> you have established;
> what are human beings that
> you are mindful of them,
> mortals that you care for them?
> Yet you have made them
> a little lower than God,
> and crowned them with glory and honor.
> You have given them dominion
> over the work of your hands,
> you have put all things under their feet. (Psalm 8:3–6)

In this psalm, humankind is nestled within creation, but given dominion over creation by the creator. It is dominion "on behalf of" and not dominion "by right." Human dominion is to be dominion in the way of God, and as both Genesis 1 and Psalm 104 make clear, dominion in the way of God is dominion exercised through blessing and caretaking. Christian spirituality will always involve blessing and caretaking, blessing and caretaking that extend to the non-human world as well as the human world.

Now for a few questions to ponder before we move to consider what a Christian spirituality might look like that is grounded in the ethos and ethics of Jesus.

1. Where thinking begins is a strong clue as to where thinking will take you. Do you agree that starting our thinking about spirituality "in the beginning" is wiser than starting with the creation of men and women in God's image? Why or why not?

2. In what ways might the notion of "parity" between humans and non-humans with respect to the care God gives to creation expand the missionary agenda of the church?

3. Is the notion of a creation-centered theology/spirituality as opposed to a human-centered theology/spiritually meaningful to you or not? Why?

4. How might "respect for life" as a core spiritual value impact both personal spirituality and communal spirituality?

5. In what ways is it clear that vis-à-vis creation, humans have not often exercised dominion in the way of God?

6. What are some possible words or metaphors that might describe the human relation to creation better than "dominion"?

Christian Spirituality as Practicing the Rule of God

The heart of a Christian theology and practice of spirituality must be Jesus' teaching and practice of the rule of God. Everything Jesus taught and did was grounded in his consciousness of God. For a person of Christian faith, to be spiritual is to share Jesus' God-consciousness, to participate in the ethos of Jesus, to live self-consciously under the rule of God.

Christian spirituality, while it will have much in common with other non-Christian expressions of spirituality, has one distinctive characteristic—it is grounded in what we can know of Jesus. From what has been said in previous chapters, it should be clear that a spirituality grounded in Jesus by no means leads inevitably to institutional religion with its elaborate systems of belief, theological formulations, and hierarchical structures. Indeed, if the church is mired in the Rome complex, such things may actually impede the development and practice of a Christian spirituality that follows Jesus in the Way of God

Spirituality is not about rites or rituals, although participation in Christian devotional practices may well support and nourish spirituality. Spirituality in the Way of Jesus is, as we have suggested, about choosing life in our encounter, our engagement, our connectedness with God, other people, and the non-human world. This does not happen solely, or even primarily within a religious community. Spirituality is an orientation to life that is lived out everywhere with everyone and everything. To reference the Micah 6:8 text again, Christian spirituality is doing justice, loving-kindness, and walking humbly with God.

We have said much already about choosing life as opposed to choosing death, about the ethics of Jesus, and about his understanding of the rule of God which we need not repeat here.

My intention has been simply to trace the lineaments of a creation-centered spirituality grounded in Jesus' spirituality of the rule of God and to raise questions that might further your own spiritual understanding and experience. A few final words need to be said, however, before moving on to the last chapter.

Spirituality and Love

It is foolish to think about measuring one's spirituality. It is simply not quantifiable, nor are there external signs that could be used to measure one's degree of spirituality. Indeed, it is possible to be spiritual and have little consciousness of it. Jesus' story of the great judgment in Matthew 25 is a case in point. According to the story, at the great judgment, the Son of Man will separate those who have followed the rule of God from those who have not. Then he will say to the former, "Come, you that are blessed by my Father, inherit the kingdom prepared for you from the foundation of the world; for I was hungry and you gave me food, I was thirsty and you gave me something to drink, I was a stranger and you welcomed me, I was naked and you gave me clothing, I was sick and you took care of me, I was in prison and you visited me'" (25:34–36).

The surprising part of the story is that the "righteous" have not recognized the significance of their compassion. They were living spiritually without recognizing it. "When, Lord," they ask him, "did we do all this to you?" His answer is full of deep wisdom: "Truly I tell you, just as you did it to one of the least of these who are members of my family, you did it to me" (25:31ff.). In a world where all creatures are *inspirited* with the very Spirit of God, all acts of compassion, kindness, justice, and love are done in the Spirit to the Spirit. The most spiritual of people may be blissfully unaware of their spirituality—although I suspect others would know of it.

Although spirituality cannot be quantified or measured, that doesn't stop people from trying. Nor does it stop them from taking pride in what they take to be signs of their spiritual accomplishments. Pride, of course, is a good sign that one's spirituality is largely undeveloped.

Apparently the Christians in Corinth were in conflict over so-called spiritual gifts, such things as speaking in tongues, healing, uttering prophecies or wisdom or knowledge, miracles, the discernment of spirits. Apparently they were arguing over a hierarchy of gifts and making judgments about each other's "spirituality" based upon what "gifts" one manifested or did not manifest. Paul, without denying the validity of such things, argued that they were not grounds for pride; rather, their purpose was the common good of the community.

Paul then tells them that he will show them a "more excellent way" than the manifestation of such spiritual gifts in the community, and in doing so he illumines the heart of a developed spirituality:

> If I speak in the tongues of mortals and of angels, but do not have love, I am a noisy gong or a clanging cymbal. And if I have prophetic powers, and understand all mysteries and all knowledge, and if I have all faith, so as to remove mountains, but do not have love, I am nothing. If I give away all my possessions, and if I hand over my body so that I may boast, but do not have love, I gain nothing. . . . And now faith, hope, and love abide, these three; and the greatest of these is love. (1 Corinthians 13:1–3, 13)

Love is greater than faith and hope because love is the content of faith and hope. Faith and hope emptied of love may still be faith and hope in something, but they are not Christian faith and hope. Love is the beating heart of Christian spirituality for love was the beating heart of everything Jesus said and did. Paul knew that. To those who insist on external signs of religious commitment, he declares that nothing matters except faith working through love (Galatians 5:6b). To the Christians in Rome, he urges them to "Owe no one anything, except to love one another; for the one who loves another has fulfilled the law. . . . Love does no wrong to a neighbor; therefore, love is the fulfilling of the law" (Romans 13:8, 10). On this point the Apostle Paul has deeply understood Jesus.

Love, not just any love but the love of God, expressed in love of God's creation is at the heart of Jesus' ministry of God's rule. When you practice the rule of God, which is the rule of love, your understanding of God and yourself deepens. 1 John 4 drives the point inescapably home:

> Beloved, let us love one another, because love is from God; everyone who loves is born of God and knows God. Whoever does not love does not know God, for God is love. *God's love was revealed* among us in this way: God sent his only Son into the world *so that we might live through him.* (1 John 4:7–9, emphasis added)

Love has an epistemic function; it is a way of knowing God. Indeed, for the author of 1 John, there is no knowing of God without love. In the experience of love—which must be understood as both loving and being loved—God is experienced as the ground of one's spiritual life. "*God is love, and those who abide in love abide in God, and God abides in them*" (1 John 4:16b, emphasis added). To love is to discover and become who you are "in God" as a spiritual person.

This love which was disclosed in the teaching and practice of Jesus is not an abstract concept or a religious duty—it is a way of being in the world that develops and expands as one experiences its reality in concrete situations and relationships. It is to be experienced in all the vicissitudes of life, which is why Paul observes that those of a Christian spirit, "rejoice with those who rejoice, weep with those who weep" (Romans 12:15). Love, of course, is more than a display of empathy; love does what can be done to enhance the joy or alleviate the suffering of the other.

Love is a correlative of that profound respect for life that we mentioned in the early part of the chapter. As such, love does not discriminate. Recall the story of the rich young man. According to Mark 10:21, "Jesus, looking at him, loved him." Recall, as well, Jesus' instructions to his followers to "Love your enemies and pray for those who persecute you,[45] so that you may be children of your Father in heaven; for he makes his sun rise on the evil and on the good, and sends rain on the righteous and on the unrighteous" (Matthew 5:44–45). From all of this we can conclude that in terms of Christian spirituality, love is not what you do; it is who you are. Becoming ever more deeply aware of and open to this truth is the only reason for following so-called spiritual practices such as meditation, prayer, devotion, community worship, acts of service, and so on. To do such things for "spiritual" self-aggrandizement is the work of the ego, not the work of God's spirit within us.

Where does all this lead us? Perhaps simply to this conclusion: to be spiritual, you (your ego) must let the Spirit be the Spirit. For many, to be spiritual is to *possess* the Spirit, to *have* the Spirit. As they are with most other things, such folks feel the need to be in control of the Spirit. But once you think you control the Spirit, what you are controlling is not the Spirit. The enlivening Spirit of God within us cannot be controlled. We must give up control and accept our fundamental existential vulnerability. Such vulnerability, which the ego so dislikes, is essential to the life of the spirit. Vulnerability, we should remember, is a function of trust, a core value in the ethos of Jesus. Or as Paul said, "If we live by the Spirit, let us also be guided by the Spirit" (Galatians 5:25).

Now, a few questions to ponder before delving into the last chapter and some final thoughts about God.

1. The suggestions in this book point more to a "Jesus-oriented" rather than a "Christ-centric" spirituality and rule out a "church-centric" spirituality. How might a Jesus-oriented spirituality be reconciled with a Christ-centered spirituality?

2. If a church-centered spirituality is ruled out, what is the role of the church in Christian spirituality?

3. What are the ways in which Christians might attempt to quantify and measure spirituality?

4. What dangers are posed to both individual Christians and the church in such attempts?

5. Is love, as discussed in this book, sufficient for grounding a Christian theology of spirituality? Why or why not?

6. If the Spirit cannot be controlled, what are the implications for the church whose *modus vivendi* is largely about control?

9. What Do You Say God Is?

We have ventured to say much about God as we have sought to trace God's footsteps in the events of human history and personal experience through the pages of this book. It is perhaps time to sum up things and see where we are in our journey into mystery, into the unknown that we seek to know and that seeks to be known.

We spoke of "correspondence" between creator and creature as grounding both divine revelation and human receptivity. We spoke about panhuman experiences of the numinous and posited a spiritual reality, an innate, if often undeveloped, human awareness or intuition of the sacred in itself and within creation. We spoke about the creative, enlivening, inspiriting presence and power of God "in the beginning" resulting in the whole creation—not just human-kind—being brought into being and animated by the Spirit of God. And in so doing, we have stretched the limits of human language in attempting to speak about the ineffable. As it is said in the opening lines of the *Tao Te Ching,* "The Tao that can be told is not the eternal Tao. The name that can be named is not the eternal Name."[1]

And so we have stressed the importance of Jesus' God-consciousness as a disclosure of God that reveals some of what is hidden, while acknowledging that although God will never be less than the revelation of God in Jesus, God will always be more than the revelation of God in Jesus. That being said, our quest to understand the Way of Jesus has given us a language and interpretive categories for exploring our own, hopefully expanding, consciousness of and experience of God. Our exploration of Jesus' teaching and practice of the rule (kingdom) of God, and the resulting ethos, provided us with tools to critique both our own individual spirituality and that of institutional religion in such a way that could lead to increased credibility and relevance for Christian faith and practice in our culturally and religiously pluralistic world.

Images of God Matter

One wonders if the seemingly common experience of the "absence of God," or the "silence of God" stems, not from any absence or silence of God, but from the fact that we neither see nor hear God because we are looking and listening for a God who does not exist. Perhaps we relate more to our images of God than to God. Our images of God may just get in the way of our experience of God. This account by Karen Armstrong of her experience as a Christian nun gets right to the point:

> I wrestled with myself in prayer, trying to force my mind to encounter God, but he remained a stern taskmaster who observed my every infringement of the Rules, or was tantalizingly absent. The more I read about the raptures of the saints, the more of a failure I felt. I was unhappily aware that what little religious experience I had, had somehow been manufactured by myself as I worked upon my feelings and imagination. Sometimes a sense of devotion was an aesthetic response to the beauty of the Gregorian chant and the liturgy. But nothing actually happened to me from a source beyond myself. I never glimpsed the God described by the prophets and mystics . . .[2]

Could it not be that her image of God as a "stern taskmaster" stood between her and the God "described by the prophets and mystics"? Images of God drawn from the Pauline and post-Pauline legal understanding of the atonement have in large part "silenced" images of God that emerged from Jesus' experience of God. In this book, we have tried to reclaim some of those images for post-modern faith.

It can be very instructive to pay attention to how people from outside the Christian tradition view what's going on within the Christian church, particularly with respect to images of God and the impact those images have on human experience. Thomas H. Fang, a Chinese scholar versed not only in Chinese thought but in Western Christian thought as well, has described the ethos of the church which stems from juridical images of God as a "medieval way of living."

> Now what is the medieval way of living? Let us read together a beautiful passage in that great work on the Italian Renaissance by J. A. Symonds. "During the Middle Ages human beings lived enveloped in a cowl. They had not seen the beauty of the world, or had seen it only to cross themselves, and turn aside and tell their beads and pray. Like St. Bernard traveling along the shores of the Lake Leman, and noticing neither the azure of the waters, nor the luxuriance of the vines, nor the radiance of the mountains with their robe of sun and snow, but bending a thought-burdened forehead over the neck of his mule; even like this monk, humanity had passed, a careful pilgrim, intent on the terrors of sin, death, and judgment, along the highways of the world, and scarcely known that they were sight worthy or that life is a blessing. Beauty is a snare, pleasure a sin, the world is a fleeting show, human beings fallen and lost, death the only certainty, judgment inevitable, hell everlasting, heaven hard to win; ignorance is acceptable to God as a proof of faith and submission; abstinence and mortification are

the only safe rules of life: these were the fixed ideas of the ascetic medieval church."[3]

This may well sound unreal to us. Long gone is the cowl that covers the eyes of the travelers walking along the shores of the Lake Leman. But for many Christians in our post-modern world, images of God inferred from the church's teaching that "human beings are fallen and lost, death is punishment for sin, judgment is inevitable, hell is everlast-ing, even heaven is hard to win" either drive them out of the church or deprive them of the spiritual joy that should emerge from the teaching and practice of the one who declared, "I have said these things to you so that my joy may be in you, and that your joy may be complete" (John 15:11).

In opposition to what he has called "a medieval way of living," Professor Yang urges us to develop an alternative view of life, one informed by his Chinese philosophical and religious backgrounds. He suggests that:

> What we now really want and what we can heartily appreciate, especially in philosophical contemplation, is a different picture of human existence, in which the full-ness of life, richness of sensibility, the charm of youth, the strength of love, the loveliness of body, the virility of spirit, the dignity of thought, the nobleness of action, the freedom of creation: all of these that pertain to the beauty of the world and the glory of human being are actually realized."[4]

This may seem like a glorification of humanity at the expense of God, but is it? It certainly leads to different images of God than those which informed the "medieval way of living." Implicit in this affirmation of humanity is an affirmation of the God of love and beauty who created and inspirited this marvelous universe for human beings and all creatures to inhabit.

Not Who, but What (How) Is God?

There are many more stories that could be cited to direct our thoughts to questions about the images of God that influence the direction of our religious thought and experience. It may well be, however, that asking the question "*Who* is God?" may be the problem. When we ask *who* God is, we tend to begin thinking of God in personal terms. When we meet a stranger, one of the first questions we ask is "Who are you?" By that question we show an interest in many things. We want to know the stranger's name, but also where he or she is from, what he or she does for a living, even what he or she believes. We are interested in their personality and character and, at a deeper level of relationship, wanting to know "Who are you?" implies an interest in the other's inner life, his or her attitudes and feelings; hopes and dreams; fears and worries; intentions and purposes. All these questions are related to the stranger's personhood. Of course, the immediacy of the person standing before you enables you to ask your questions and receive an answer.

But when you ask the question, "Who are you, God?" the most immediate answer will be silence. God is not immediately present to you to receive and answer your questions in the same manner that the stranger is. Furthermore, most of the "personal" questions you might ask of a stranger do not seem applicable to God.

As to asking about God's name, we are still in a quandary. In human religion, God goes by many names. Jews and Christians have several names for the divine, among them Yahweh, Adonai, Elohim, and simply God; Muslims call the divine Allah; Confucianists use the name Heaven; the name is Ngi for the Kikuyu and Nzambi for the Bakongo in Africa; Hindu believers call upon the divine with the names Shiva, Vishnu, Brahma, and Shakti; for the Ojibwa people of North America, the sacred is Manitou or Great Spirit.

Remember, however, the wisdom of the *Tao Te Ching*, "The name that can be named is not the eternal Name."

Recall the story of Moses in the wilderness tending the flock of his father-in-law at Mount Horeb, the "mountain of God" (Exodus 3ff.). Suddenly, he sees "a flame of fire [coming] out of a bush; he looked, and the bush was blazing, yet it was not consumed." He is overcome with curiosity and draws closer to it and is told to take off his shoes for he is standing on "holy ground" (3:5). In this visionary experience, Moses is commissioned by God to return to Egypt and lead the Hebrew slaves to freedom and to the promise long ago made to Abraham and Sarah of a land and a nation. Before setting off on his mission, however, he asks God to tell him God's name because, as he puts it to God: "If I come to the Israelites and say to them, 'The God of your ancestors has sent me to you,' and they ask me, 'What is his name?' What shall I tell them?" (3:13). With his question, Moses is drawn into an "ontological divine mystery of the most daunting character."[5] God responds to Moses' request with a name that is not really a name; it is a verb: *'Ehyeh-'Asher-'Ehyeh.* This Hebrew expression can be translated in various ways: I Am-Who-I-Am, I-Am-That-I-Am, or I-Will-Be-Who-(or What)-I-Will-Be. It is "also possible to construe this as "I am He who Endures."[6]

After giving Moses a name that is not a name, God says to him, "Thus you shall say to the Israelites, 'I AM ('Ehyeh) has sent me to you'" (3:14). This does not mean that human beings cannot call upon their deity by whatever name embodies their devotion, their longings, their experience of the divine. It does mean, however, that God is more than the name with which human beings invoke God.

We are not done with the encounter between Moses and I AM. Before releasing Moses to his task, God also said to him, "Thus you shall say to the Israelites, 'The LORD (I AM), the God of your ancestors, the God of Abraham, the God of Isaac, and the God of Jacob, has sent me to you'" (3:15). Which is to say, "That-which-is-before-and-after the promises to your ancestors has sent me to you." Here we stand before the God beyond our projections and images, the God who transcends our attempts to name and define God, but whose hiddenness is at least partially disclosed in the events of human history—chief among them for Christians, as we have noted, in the Exodus and in the life, death, and post-crucifixion appearances of Jesus of Nazareth.

Whenever we attempt to define God or to ascribe attributes to God we come up against the limits of both human language and human intellect and imagination. As T. S. Eliot put it:

Words strain,
Crack and sometimes break, under the burden,
Under the tension, slip, slide, perish,
Decay with imprecision, will not stay in place,
Will not stay still. (*The Four Quartets: Burnt Norton*)[7]

Nevertheless, speak of God we must, but our speaking must be done with a keen awareness that our words are not God. Our words cannot contain God, and if we ever think they can, then we have lost God altogether. Our words about God are no more than attempts to interpret experiences of the divine and to lay the grounds for further exploration of this great mystery. As a Zen aphorism would put it, the finger pointing at the moon is not the moon.

So speak of God we will, but bear in mind the analogical nature of what is said. We are seeking to find some similarities among realities that in most respects appear to be dissimilar. As an attempt to avoid the slippery slope of *over* personalizing or anthropomorphizing our images of God, we will ask not "Who is God?" but rather, "What (or even how) is God?" The focus is then more on how God is experienced rather than on God as God is in God's self. We are seeking to understand ways in which God is active in relation to us and in doing so to catch a glimpse of something in God that moves God to relate in gracious and caretaking ways to all that is not God.

Before delineating a few images that speak more to "how" God is in human experience than "who" God is in God's self, let's stop to reflect on the following questions:

1. In what ways does our quest to understand Jesus' teaching and practice of the rule of God give us (or not give us) a language and interpretive categories for exploring our own consciousness and experiences of God?

2. Can images of God drawn from Jesus' experience of God and images of God drawn from a Pauline legal understanding of the atonement be reconciled? If so, how? If not, why not?

3. Does Professor Fang's characterization of the "medieval way of living" ring true or not true? Why?

4. In what ways, if at all, does a "medieval way of living" manifest itself in contemporary Christian culture?

5. Theologically, psychologically, and practically, how might asking "how" God is rather than "who" God is impact both personal and communal spirituality?

What (or How) Is God?

Wondering what and how God is in the world brings us to the words Spirit and spirit. Spirit points to the "what," to God as vital principle, the *élan vital*, the creative life force, or animating force within creation, while spirit points us to the "how," the essential principle, the essence of God's activity in the world. What follows continues our summing up of major themes in this book.

God Is Spirit

In John 4:24, Jesus declares in conversation with a Samaritan woman, "God is Spirit." It is clear from the gospels, however, that Jesus has more in mind than an impersonal energy or force that both creates the natural world and is the principle of causation and evolution in the natural world. For Jesus, to say God is Spirit seems to mean that God is *incorporeal consciousness.* Although once again our language fails us, we are to understand that in Jesus' experience, God is revealed as having the attributes of consciousness: awareness, intelligence, thought, will, intentionality.

The presence of God as Spirit, as incorporeal consciousness, is affirmed in the New Testament gospel narratives. His mother, Mary, is said to have conceived him "from the Holy Spirit" (Matthew 1:20). After his baptism by John the Baptist, "the Spirit descended on him" (Mark 1:10). It was "the Spirit that drove him out into the wilderness" to go through a rigorous preparation for his ministry (Mark 1:12). When he delivered his mission manifesto in his home town of Nazareth, he declared "the Spirit of the Lord is upon me" (Luke 4:18). It is "by the Spirit of God" that he casts out demons (Matthew 12:28). He "rejoiced in the Holy Spirit, thanking God for revealing to him things 'hidden from the wise and the intelligent'" (Luke 10:21). From beginning to end, Jesus carries out his teaching and practice of God's rule accompanied by the Spirit, inspired by the Spirit, enlightened by the Spirit, and empowered by the Spirit.

God Is the Spirit of Creativity

We have seen how the Spirit hovered over chaos "in the beginning" as God brought the world we know into being. We affirm that creation was not a once-for-all event, but rather is on going. Creation is not a clock—made, wound up, left to run until it runs down. Creation, what we would take to be the "necessary" work of the Spirit, once begun continues in the evolution of the universe and in the evolution of life forms.

One of the ways in which the correspondence between Spirit and humankind can be seen is in human creativity. It is interesting how works of magnificent artistry, be it a symphony, a painting, or a poem, are often characterized as "divine." Human artistic creativity, as well as scientific and technological ingenuity, and the creation of political, economic, and cultural institutions that "choose life," reflect (and perhaps embody) the Spirit of Creativity that is God.

God Is the Spirit of Renewal

All things grow old with the passage of time. Civilizations and everything in them rise and fall. The once vital lose vitality and move toward dissolution. And so it is of all living creatures as well—the cycle of birth, growth, decline, and death. Everything that arises persists for a while and then falls away. As Buddhism teaches, all things are temporal, transient, impermanent. To take Paul a bit out of context, "the creation was subjected to futility, not of its own will but by the will of the one who subjected it, in hope . . ." (Romans 8:20).

What is the "hope" of creation? The immediate hope of renewal and the eschatological hope of re-creation (cf. Revelation 21:1–6). We discussed renewal in the opening chapter and pointed to the promise of the renewing Spirit that, "As long as the earth endures, seedtime and harvest, cold and heat, summer and winter, day and night, shall not cease" (Genesis 8:22). In chapter 8 we saw with respect to living creatures that:

> These all look to you
> to give them their food in due season;
> when you give to them, they gather it up;
> when you open your hand, they are filled
> with good things.
> When you hide your face, they are dismayed;
> when you take away their breath, they die
> and return to their dust.
> *When you send forth your spirit, they are created;*
> *and you renew the face of the ground.*
> (Psalm 104:27–30, emphasis added)

It could be argued—to use the language of Genesis—that humans are correctly exercising their "dominion" when they engage in acts of renewal. Each time we plant the fields, cultivate, harvest, and replant, we are renewing the face of the earth. Each death and each new birth is a renewal. Each struggle to revitalize exhausted, devitalized, dispirited institutions that no longer serve the wholeness and well-being of people and/or the natural environment is a renewal of the face of the earth. Each scientific and technological advancement that enhances previously diminished life is a renewal. We are acting in correspondence with Spirit when our efforts bring about some form of renewal.

God Is the Spirit of Truth

To say that God is the Spirit of Truth is not an invitation to abstract philosophical or theological speculation on "truth." It does, however, involve us in practical questions of ethical importance. It is not without reason that the Gospel of John expresses the faith of the early church by having Jesus declare, "I am the way, and the *truth,* and the life" (John 14:6, emphasis added). There are many ethical considerations to be drawn from Jesus' understanding of the rule of God, but chief among them is the truth we pointed to in chapter 8 that Spirit does not discriminate in its caretaking of creation. Love does not discriminate (Matthew 5:43ff.). The notion that some are worthy and some are not is antithetical to Spirit and thus the work of what Jesus called "the father of lies" (John 8:44). That God does not discriminate was not an obvious truth for Jesus' contemporaries who believed that God had a "preferential option" for the Jews, and it seems not to be an obvious truth to many Christians who harbor beliefs of "predestination" and "manifest destiny."

God as the Spirit of Truth, however, tells a different story. Contrary to what we might desire, God has no preference for special nations and peoples. One need only read the Acts 10 account of how Peter learned the "truth" from the Spirit of Truth that he "should not call anyone profane or unclean" (Acts 10:28). Peter had come to understand that "God shows no partiality" (Acts 10:34). It was the Spirit who told Peter not to make discriminatory distinctions (Acts 11:12). The same truth is reflected in Paul's proclamation that discriminatory distinctions between Jew and Greek, slave and free, male and female have no place in a Christian world view because all are "one in Christ" (Galatians 3:28).

Whenever people work to dismantle the "isms" that plague our world, for example, racism, sexism, ageism, and classism, their work is an expression of the Spirit of Truth. Whenever people work to dismantle the power structures that exploit, oppress, or brutalize some people for the benefit of other people, their work is an expression of the Spirit of Truth. And it must be said that whoever does this "work," regardless of their religious commitments, is worshipping the Spirit in "spirit and in truth" (John 4:23–24).

God Is the Spirit of Justice

To say that God is the Spirit of Truth is akin to saying that God is the Spirit of Justice. The truth we just mentioned demands justice, that is, fairness, equitableness, parity with respect to those things that make life "abundant" (John 10:10). The rule of God is egalitarian. This is the untiring message of the prophets of ancient Israel.

To give just two examples, over against the rampant social and economic injustices of his society, the Prophet Isaiah declares that God is "laying in Zion a foundation stone, a tested stone, a precious cornerstone, a sure foundation. . . . And [he] will make justice the line, and righteousness the plummet; [and] hail will sweep away the refuge of lies . . ." (Isaiah 28:16–17). And as we mentioned in chapter 5, according to the prophet Amos, God is not interested in, indeed God detests, the worship of people who tolerate or practice injustice and waits for the day when "justice [will] roll down like waters, and righteousness like an ever-flowing stream" (Amos 5:24).

Clearly justice as envisioned by the Spirit of Justice has little to do with legal definitions and codes of justice that prevail in most human societies. Such legal codes often, in the name of justice, legally sanction attitudes, values, and behaviors that radically contradict justice viewed through the prism of the rule of God. Whenever men and women work in favor of, and are willing to suffer and perhaps even die for, justice understood as simple fairness, equitableness, and parity among peoples in the things that enhance human dignity and well-being, they are standing on the "foundation stone" established by the Spirit of Justice.

God Is the Spirit of Counsel

To call God the Spirit of Counsel is to evoke more than one image. Most people when faced with difficult and complex realities will seek the "counsel" of others, particularly those whose knowledge or expertise in the area of difficulty or complexity is greater than their own. In the business world, we might seek the advice of fellow professionals; in our personal lives we might seek the counsel of friends or family members. In some cases we might seek the counsel of a pastor, a social worker, or a psychiatrist—individuals who are often referred to as "counselors." These are all people who can give us advice, help us solve problems, open new perspectives for us, provide new insights. Such folks, be they family, friends, or professionals, also serve as "truth tellers," that is, their counsel can help guard against the human tendency for self-deception and moral blindness.

Those with some wisdom will seek counsel from family, friends, colleagues, or professionals when they perceive its necessity for them. Sometimes counsel is offered when it has not been sought; those with some wisdom will pay attention and take it into account. In either case, counsel as positive advice, guidance, direction, and truth-telling is something we all understand and, if we are fortunate, experience. God as the Spirit of Counsel fulfills this function for those who are open to it.

In John 14, Jesus promises his followers just such a "spiritual" counselor when he tells them:

> I will ask the Father, and he will give you another Advocate (helper) to be with you forever. This is the Spirit of truth, whom the world cannot receive, because it neither sees him nor knows him. You know him, because he abides with you, and *he will be in you*. . . . the Advocate (helper), the Holy Spirit, whom the Father will send in my name,

will teach you everything, and remind you of all that I
have said to you." (John 14:16–17, 26, emphasis added)

Christian experience of the indwelling of the Spirit of
Counsel has been the impetus for prayers seeking advice
and direction in making decisions as to how to live faith-
fully under the rule of God in the day-to-day world. The
meaning of counsel, however, goes beyond seeking advice
and direction.

When we are hurt, grieving, anxious, or feeling lost,
we seek the counsel of others for encouragement, comfort,
and consolation. God as the Spirit of Counsel brings such
comfort and consolation to both the community of faith
and individuals. In Acts 9:31, Luke tells of how the church
lived "in the comfort of the Spirit," and Paul declares that
God is "the Father of mercies and the God of all consolation, who consoles us in all our affliction, so that we may be
able to console those who are in any affliction with the consolation with which we ourselves are consoled by God" (2
Corinthians 1:3–4). Both in public worship and in private
devotion, it is characteristic of Christian people to seek the
encouragement, comfort, and consolation of God, the Spirit
of Counsel, and to extend such divine consolation to others
who are afflicted in any way.

We have not yet exhausted the meaning of counsel. The
words *counsel* and *counselor* are also legal terms and are used
as synonyms for attorneys, for those who "advocate" on behalf
of others. It is in this sense that Paul states that, "the Spirit
helps us in our weakness; for we do not know how to pray as
we ought, but that very Spirit intercedes with sighs too deep
for words" (Romans 8:26). It is interesting to note that God,
as the Spirit of Counsel, advocates not only on our behalf, but
also on behalf of Jesus. "When the Advocate comes, whom
I will send to you from the Father, the Spirit of truth who
comes from the Father, he will testify on my behalf" (John
15:26).

Each of these meanings of counsel that can be found in an English dictionary are also contained within the Greek words *parakaleo* (verb) and *parakletos* (noun) which are often used in the New Testament to describe the Spirit's activity with respect to both individuals and communities of faith. More than anything else, I suspect that it is confidence in God as the Spirit of Counsel that moves Christians to petitionary and intercessory prayer and action. When Christian men and women are counselors in the full meaning of the term to each other and to those outside the community of Christian faith, they become the occasion for those others to experience God as the Spirit of Counsel.

God Is the Spirit of Compassion

Over and again, Jesus, the revealer of God, is described in the Gospels as having "compassion" and mercy. His compassion was undiscriminating. One of the most poignant texts in the Gospels shows Jesus expressing his compassion for the people who were about to kill him: "Jerusalem, Jerusalem, the city that kills the prophets and stones those who are sent to it! How often have I desired to gather your children together as a hen gathers her brood under her wings, and you were not willing!" (Matthew 23:37). Even during the agony of crucifixion he continued to express compassion when he advocated for all those complicit in his death: "Father forgive them; for they do not know what they are doing" (Luke 23:34).

If human religious traditions emerge from the panhuman quest for the numinous, then thematic correspondence between the traditions is to be expected. That is certainly the case with respect to compassion/mercy. To give one striking example, *tz'u*, compassion/mercy is a Chinese concept deeply rooted in the religious consciousness of Buddhist devotees. Used with other words, the meaning of mercy and compassion is deepened, for example, *tz'u pei*, which combines *tz'u* (mercy and compassion) with *pei* (a heart of pity, sympathy, or sadness). The emphases becomes "pity for another in distress and the desire to help that person." Other examples would be *tz'u hsin*, a compassionate heart, *tz'u yi*, the mind of compassion, and *tz'u yen*, the compassionate eye.[8] When the word *pei* (pity, sympathy) is combined with *yuan* (vow), you have a term which expresses the "the great pitying vow of Buddhas and bodhisattvas to save all beings."[9] Indeed, the term bodhisattva refers to an enlightened being who, out of compassion, forgoes entry into Nirvana until all beings are enlightened. It is correct to say that Buddhism, particularly in its Mahayana expressions, revolves around the theme of compassion or mercy (*tz'u pei*). It stems from the Buddhist religious insight that life is suffering and that compassion is necessary in enabling people to journey though this life of suffering (*samsara*) to finally reach eternal bliss (*nirvana*).

In Christianity as well as in Buddhism, the theme of compassion/mercy elucidates the relationship between God and humankind and God and the non-human world. God is experienced as the Spirit of Compassion, and it is here that we can so clearly see how our different linguistic attempts to describe the numinous collapse into each other. God as the Spirit of Compassion is the Spirit of Creativity, and the Spirit of Renewal, and the Spirit of Truth, and the Spirit of Justice, and the Spirit of Counsel, and all together express the fundamental truth of Christian faith and experience: God is Love.

When people look upon each other with compassion, the Spirit of Compassion looks through their eyes and to be spiritual is to look upon the world with compassion. When describing God's caretaking of creation, God's undiscriminating love for all people, Jesus told his followers that they were to "Be perfect, therefore, as your heavenly Father is perfect" (Matthew 5:48). Given the context, the text could be translated as "Be compassionate as your heavenly Father is compassionate."

A Child's Meditation on God

How, then, should we conclude our reflections on God? Jesus said that the rule of God belonged to children (Mark 10:14). Perhaps, then, a poem on God by a child would be most appropriate. With these simple, but certainly profound words, Gayatri Lobo Gajiwala, a twelve-year-old girl from Indonesia, expressed her sense of God as Spirit:

> To me, God is a diary
> To whom I can tell all
> To whom when I'm in trouble
> I can very easily call.
>
> From whom I have nothing to hide
> To whom I can easily show
> Every single bit of me
> For She already knows.
>
> To Her I can tell my story
> No matter how short or long
> I can tell Her everything
> Whether it's right or wrong.
>
> But unlike the usual diary
> What I tell Her no one knows
> For after I have finished
> My book is shut tight—closed.
>
> Then when I want to talk to Her
> I have a special key
> This key is really important
> And it is reserved only for me.

And maybe God is your diary too
And you have your special key
But even if you don't, be sure
God is still there for you and me.[10]

This is a prayer from the heart of a twelve-year-old girl, innocent, sincere and simple, but filled with powerful images and metaphors that make it rather extraordinary. "God is a diary," says the prayer. This diary is a life story told in the privacy of the spirit. This diary consists of the happenings, thoughts, and reflections that take place between a human spirit and the divine Spirit. It reflects the human longing for the divine Spirit. It is filled with the hopes and despairs, tears and laughter that the diarist "writes into" God. The diary also contains the responses of God that pave the way in the diarist's life journey. In short, the diary is a metaphor for the conversation between a human person and God in the fellowship of spirit with Spirit. Without the "correspondence" between spirit and Spirit, the conversation is not possible.

The prayer of this little girl speaks of "a special key" to open the diary. What is this special key? We are not told explicitly. All she says is that the special key "is really important." We can, however, venture the guess that if the diary is God, then what opens the diary for the little girl to record her life is the divine will to love expressed throughout creation in the ubiquity of Spirit. God as Spirit is the "key." Not God as a theological construction, not God affirmed in the belief systems and creeds of the varying churches and religions, not God handed down by religious traditions and authorities, but God as Spirit, the Spirit that was "in the beginning," that inspirits all creation, and that, as Jesus noted, blows freely like the wind where it will (John 3:8). Without this Spirit, our prayer would not be a conversation between us and God. It would no more than a sad and futile monologue, no more than our talking to ourselves.

Notes

Chapter One

1. This creation hymn is found in *Rig Veda*, X, 129. See Mircea Eliade, *From Primitives to Zen: A Thematic Sourcebook of the History of Religions* (London: Collins/Fount Paperbacks, 1977), 86.
2. The story is told by Tway La' and transcribed by Huang Tung-chiou in Wu Min-yi, ed., *Origins* (Tourism Office/Taiwan Ministry of Transportation, 1992), 27–29.
3. Claus Westermann, *Genesis 1-11, A Commentary* (Minneapolis: Augsburg, 1984), 395. This is an important observation as Christian biblical scholars have principally made comparative studies only between the Genesis story of the flood and the Assyrian version of the flood story found in the Gilgamesh epic.
4. Ibid.
5. S. Thompson, *Folklore: Theories and Allocations*, vol. 2 (Tokyo: Sekai Sisosha, 1977), 31.
6. John Bunyan, *The Pilgrim's Progress* (New York: Airmont Publishing Company, Inc., 1969), 17 (emphasis added).
7. Walter Brueggemann, *Genesis: A Bible Commentary for Teaching and Preaching* (Louisville: John Knox Press, 1982), 175.

Chapter Two

1. Cf. Morna D. Hooker, *A Commentary on the Gospel According to St. Mark* (London: A & C Black, 1991), 382.
2. Gerard S. Sloyan, *John: A Bible Commentary for Teaching and Preaching* (Atlanta: John Knox Press, 1988), 221.

Chapter Three

1. Ibid.
2. E.g., Hugh Anderson, *The Gospel of Mark*, New Century Bible (London: Oliphants, 1976), 222.

Chapter Four

1. Mircea Eliade, *The Encyclopedia of Religion*, vol. 12 (New York: Macmillan, 1987), 287.
2. Christmas Humphreys, ed., *The Wisdom of Buddhism* (London: Curzon Press, 1979), 81–83.
3. C. K. Yang, *Religion in Chinese Society* (Berkeley: University of California Press, 1961), 1.
4. Ibid.
5. Paul J. Griffs, *Problems of Religious Diversity* (Massachusetts: Blackwell, 2001), 7.
6. Roberts and Donaldson, trans. (www.earlychristianwritings.com/text/didache-roberts.html), 1.
7. *San Francisco Examiner*, 7 Nov. 1999, sec. A, 21, 26.
8. *San Francisco Chronicle*, 8 Nov. 1999, sec. A, 10.
9. Yang, 296.
10. Achiel Peelman, *Christ Is a Native American* (Maryknoll: Orbis Books, 1995), 22.

Chapter Five

1. Kenneth L. Woodward, *Newsweek*, Dec. 31/Jan. 7, 2002, 102.
2. Ibid., 105.

Chapter Six

1. Samuel High Moffett, *A History of Christianity in Asia*, vol. 1 (New York: Harper San Francisco, 1992), 506.
2. *The American Heritage Dictionary of the English Language*, 3rd ed. (Boston: Houghton Mifflin Company, 1992), s.v. "ethos."
3. Ibid.
4. John Dominic Crossan, *Jesus: A Revolutionary Biography* (New York: HarperCollins, 1995), 66.
5. Ibid., 48.
6. Robert H. Smith, *Matthew: Augsburg Commentary on the New Testament* (Minneapolis: Augsburg, 1989), 81.
7. Craig L. Bloomberg, *Matthew: New American Commentary*, vol. 22 (Nashville: Broadman Press, 1992), 98.
8. Ibid., 100.

Chapter Seven

1. *The American Heritage Dictionary of the English Language,* 3rd ed. (Boston: Houghton Mifflin Company, 1992), s.v. "complex."
2. Many scholars concur that the "year of the Lord's favor" is a reference to the "year of Jubilee" (Leviticus 25) when the economic playing ground is leveled as debt is forgiven and land is returned to impoverished families who had lost it as collateral. For example, see David Tiede, *Luke* (Minneapolis: Augsburg, 1988), 107.
3. Thomas Cleary, trans., *Dhammapada: The Sayings of the Buddha* (New York: Bantam Books, 1994), 61.

Chapter Eight

1. C.S. Song, and Joseph D. Driskill, "Deepening Love—Practicing Justice: Spiritual Nurture for Our Time," *Reformed World,* 51, no. 1 (March 2001), 3–19.
2. Cf., Gordon J. Wenham, *Genesis 1-15,* World Biblical Commentary, vol.1 (Waco, Tex.: Word Books, 1987), 17.

Chapter Nine

1. Stephen Mitchell, trans., *Tao Te Ching* (New York: Harper and Row, 1988), 1.
2. Karen Armstrong, *A History of God: The 4,000 Year Quest of Judaism, Christianity and Islam* (New York: Ballantine Books, 1993), xviii.
3. Thomas H. Fang, *The Chinese View of Life: The Philosophy of Comprehensive Harmony* (Taipei: Linking Publishing Co., 1980), 58–59.
4. Ibid.
5. Robert Alter, *The Five Books of Moses: A Translation with Commentary* (New York: W.W. Norton & Co., 2004), 321.
6. Ibid.
7. T. S. Eliot, *Collected Poems, 1909-1962* (New York: Harcourt, Brace & World, 1963), 180.
8. William Edward Soothhill, and Lewis Hodous, comp., *A Dictionary of Chinese Buddhist Terms,* (Delhi: Motilal Banarsidass, 1937), 399.
9. Ibid., 371.
10. Gayatri Lobo Gajiwala, "God," *Journal of Asian Women's Resource Center for Culture and Theology,* 21, no. 1 (March 2002), 55.

Index